Legendary Ayrshire

Custom : Folklore : Tradition

Other books by Dane Love:

Title	Publisher
Scottish Kirkyards	Robert Hale
The History of Auchinleck – Village and Parish	Carn Publishing
Pictorial History of Cumnock	Alloway Publishing
Pictorial History of Ayr	Alloway Publishing
Scottish Ghosts	Robert Hale
Scottish Ghosts	Barnes & Noble
The Auld Inns of Scotland	Robert Hale
Guide to Scottish Castles	Lomond Books
Tales of the Clan Chiefs	Robert Hale
Scottish Covenanter Stories	Neil Wilson
Ayr Stories	Fort Publishing
Ayrshire Coast	Fort Publishing
Scottish Spectres	Robert Hale
Scottish Spectres	Ulverston Large Print
Ayrshire: Discovering a County	Fort Publishing
Ayr Past and Present	Sutton Publishing
Lost Ayrshire	Birlinn
The River Ayr Way	Carn Publishing
Ayr – the Way We Were	Fort Publishing
The Man Who Sold Nelson's Column	Birlinn
Jacobite Stories	Neil Wilson
The History of Sorn – Village and Parish	Carn Publishing
Scottish Ghosts	Amberley Books
The Covenanter Encyclopaedia	Fort Publishing

www.dane-love.co.uk

Legendary Ayrshire

Custom : Folklore : Tradition

Dane Love

CARN PUBLISHING

First Published in Great Britain, 2009.

ISBN - 978 0 9518128 6 0

Published by Carn Publishing,
Lochnoran House,
Auchinleck, Ayrshire, KA18 3JW.

Printed by Bell & Bain Ltd,
Glasgow, G46 7UQ.

Contents

List of Illustrations

Introduction

In this modern age, many of the traditional tales of our country are being forgotten and not handed down to the next generation. The internet, computers, television and a whole host of modern attractions mean that many residents of Ayrshire no longer talk about, let alone visit, the numerous historical and legendary places in the county. In some cases, with the antiquarian interest forgotten, these ancient sites are being destroyed, or at best simply neglected, through lack of knowledge.

This book is an attempt at bringing back to the general public's acquaintance some of the stories and traditions of yesteryear. Tales that were handed down from father to son, grandmother to grand-daughter, often around the fireside on a cold winter's night, have in many cases died out, and yet were the staple means of entertainment at one time.

Similarly, many ancient traditions and customs have died, and their existence no longer known about by the residents of the villages in which they were practised for centuries. Customs and traditional events may no longer be carried out by modern man, but in many communities, even the memory or recording of these ancient ceremonies no longer exists.

Ayrshire is not generally seen as being as superstitious, steeped in folklore or as interested in legends as some other Scottish counties, but the number of such customs and traditions that once existed in the area were a match for other places. This volume hopes to bring back to more prominence some of the tales of the past and, hopefully, will re-ignite an interest in these stories and locations associated with them.

Some of the legends or customs in this book are purely fanciful, such as the actions of the Devil in throwing a lump of Dailly parish into the sea, creating Ailsa Craig, whereas others were seen as being true, and the persecution of numerous women and men during the time when witchcraft was seen as being a threat to the kirk and man's morals, was all too real for many people.

I like a traditional tale, and over the years I have gathered up many interesting snippets from various people who have spoken to me about their own local area, or own specialist knowledge. Some of these tales are purely local and were handed down orally over the centuries. In many cases, the knowledge and tradition associated with certain places, be it ancient stones or wells, was in danger of being lost, today's generations seemingly showing no interest in them. And yet, having spoken to many local history groups and other organisations with an interest in the past, there is a hunger to find out more.

I hope that this book will interest the reader enough to make them more aware of the little places and strange customs that formerly held more prominence in our society. Not all historical events were tied up with great castles, ancient abbeys or battles. Often the story behind an old boulder on the open moor can be every bit as interesting, as I have found to my delight when compiling this book. Hopefully, the reader will agree with me.

Dane Love,
Auchinleck, 2009.

CHAPTER ONE

ROCKS and STONES

There is nothing more wonderful than standing by the side of some ancient standing stone or massive boulder and wondering what early man made of it – was it a place of worship, a place of burial, or somewhere that was so distinctively different that tales were made up to explain the stone's existence? Ayrshire has no great stone circles to compare with the Stones of Callanais or Brogar, indeed it hardly has a stone circle of any significance at all, but there are a number of great stones or boulders that have developed legends over the centuries.

Of the few stone circles that do exist, however, one can still be traced at Garleffin, a small clachan located on the south side of the River Stinchar at Ballantrae. At one time the circle of stones here was quite extensive, there being eight uprights dotted around the field. However, in the late eighteenth century the local farmer decided that two of the stones were hindering his work in the fields and had them removed. The others survived, but again in the twentieth century the remaining stones were getting in the way of agricultural machinery and were removed. This took place in 1991, prior to the site being scheduled by Historic Scotland. Now there are only two stones still to be seen, located in the garden of a bungalow erected in 1966. These stones have remained untouched by modern man.

The stones of Garleffin were studied by the noted archaeologist of the early nineteenth century Ludovic MacLellan Mann in 1829 and his calculations claimed that they were aligned with a solar eclipse that would have taken place at noon on 31 December 2709 BC. The stones, five upright and three fallen by 1856, formed the shape of a half ellipse, around 233 yards in length. Local tradition claimed that a battle took place on the plain at the foot of the Stinchar, and that the stones marked the graves of the buried chieftains. Although the stones were moved, their location is known, and it has been speculated that it may be possible to have them re-erected as a landscape feature, the archaeology beneath them being in situ still.

In Hastings Square, at Darvel, stands two considerable memorials, one a war memorial, the other commemorating Sir Alexander Fleming, discoverer of penicillin, who was born at Lochfield farm nearby. There is also a lesser object, a rude stone, which locals have called the 'Dagon Stone' for many years. It is covered with curious markings which some folk claim were a form of hieroglyphics, but others say that they are natural weathering marks. Nevertheless, the Darvel folk hold this stone in great reverence, and it has been a significant part of their culture for many centuries. Ludovic MacLellan Mann studied the stone in some detail and he concluded that there were to be seen on three faces of it a total of twelve small round depressions. Many of these could be linked with straight lines, and he reported that they were cut by early man according to ancient astronomical laws. He claimed that the stone was associated with the noon-day sun, particularly at mid-summer, when it was at its highest. According to Mann, the noon-day sun god was associated with life-giving power, fertility and prosperity.

On New Year's Day, after the kirk bells had rung, the folk of Darvel used to walk round the Dagon Stone three times to ensure good luck. Even the provost and councillors carried out this custom, and it is said that wedding parties followed a fiddler round the stone three times in a sun-wise direction to ensure a happy and fertile marriage.

When the Dagon Stone was upended is not known, perhaps in the Bronze Age, but there are some who claim the date to be as late as 1752, when the village street was laid out and a new roadway constructed. Certainly, the stone did not have its headpiece until 1821, for it is known that in that year a rounded stone was discovered whilst excavating a curling pond, and was placed on top of old Dagon. This was stolen and dumped in a deep pool, but the locals had become accustomed to it and managed to rescue it. The local blacksmith, William Morton, was commissioned to make a steel pin and make it secure. In 1873 the council decided that it had become a hazard to traffic and were going to have it dumped, but Alexander Mair saved it and had it erected in one of his fields as a rubbing stone for cattle. It was rescued from there and placed in the garden of the Brown's Institute until 1894 when it was relocated to the green in Burn Road. It was later moved to its present site in Hastings Square.

Another community with its own celebrated boulder is Monkton. In the centre of the village can be found the Hare Stane, perched on a man-made base of cobbles, near to the Cross. This was not the original location for this stone, for it once lay on a low hillock to the north of the village. In 2000, it was decided to have the stone relocated to the village centre. Buried below it was a 'Millennium Box', a time capsule containing items of local and national interest.

1.1 The Muckle or Hare Stane, Monkton, which was moved to its present location at the Millennium. *(Dane Love)*

The original site of the Hare Stane, or Muckle Stane of Monkton as it was also known, was on a low grassy knoll at Muirhouse, which is a farm by the side of the Kilmarnock Road, off Charles Avenue. Little tradition has been passed down concerning the stone, but it was deemed sufficiently important enough for it to be rescued from obliteration.

To the east of Muirkirk, on the farm of Lightshaw, can be seen a pointed standing stone, positioned in the middle of a roadside field. The stone has no real history associated with it, but John Smith speculated in 1895 that the name of the farm may derive from 'Laight

Shaw', being old Scots for the grave in the wood. As such, the stone would have marked the grave of some warrior chieftain. The stone is about seven feet in height, the base around three feet by two feet six inches.

There are a few stones in Scotland which are traditionally associated with feats of strength. Some of them were large boulders used as tests of strength for grown men, whereas others were used to test when boys had grown into men. Generally known as 'Lifting Stones', these can be found at various spots across the countryside. One set of stones is to be found in the kirkyard of Old Dailly, located 2½ miles

1.2 The Blue Stones of Dailly, at one time used to test a man's strength. *(Dane Love)*

east of Girvan. Here, within the old aisle of the ruinous kirk, are two rounded blue-coloured boulders. They were known locally as the Charter or Blue Stones of Dailly. From their smooth surface and weight, the lifting of these stones was regarded by the parishioners as a great feat of skill and strength and was used to determine whether lads from the locality were men. The two stones were slightly different sizes, and weigh around 280 and 340 pounds, the larger known as 'The Big Blue'.

Despite the two stones lying undisturbed in the kirkyard for at least seven hundred years, there was possibility that the stones might be stolen for their historical interest. Accordingly, in March 2001, following advice from Historic Scotland, South Ayrshire Council decided that they should be protected. As a result, two iron straps were placed round the stones and affixed to the wall. Many locals claimed that this act was 'bureaucracy gone mad', for the stones had been in the kirk since the thirteenth century, and now that they were anchored to the kirk wall, no-one in the parish would be able to try his strength out on them, thus killing an ancient tradition.

The Dailly stones are also supposed to have curative powers, and for many years people would go to the kirkyard to touch them, claiming that they had the ability to cure headaches and relieve stress. People suffering from other unspecified illnesses were said to find miracle cures simply by touching the stones, and those who were not ill could still find a feeling of well-being by rubbing the stones with their hands.

Tradition also states that the Dailly stones were stones of sanctuary, originally being placed at the altar in the church. However, Sir Walter Scott, in *The Lord of the Isles* refers to only one boulder, which he calls the Charter Stone. In a footnote Scott wrote:

> The village of New Dailly being now larger than the old place of the same name, the inhabitants insisted that the Charter Stone should be removed from the old town to the new, but the people of Old Dailly were unwilling to part with their ancient right. Demands and remonstrances were made on each side without effect, till at last, man, woman, and child of both villages marched out and by one desperate engagement put an end to a war, the commencement of which no person then living remembered. Justice and victory, in this instance, being of the same part, the villagers of the old town of Dailly now enjoy the pleasure of keeping the 'blue stane' unmolested.

Sanctuary Stones existed at various places across Scotland and were used to define the extent of the sanctuary, or place where wrongdoers could take refuge and avoid capture. One of the more famous places in Scotland to have these stones was Torphichen Preceptory in West

Lothian, where four Sanctuary Stones still mark the limit of the safe ground around the preceptory. The stones at Dailly were less elaborate than these stones, and it was said that criminals, in particular debtors, could avoid apprehension if they stood with their back against them.

Another Ayrshire village that had a lifting stane was Loans, which is now almost absorbed into Troon. By the side of the road can still be found the old lifting stane that was used by locals to test their strength.

Prestwick had an ancient Charter Stone at one time. Tradition claims that this was the charter stone of the lepers who were based at Kingcase Well, and that originally it was located adjacent to the water source. The stone comprises a block of basalt and was rounded in shape. The weight of the stone was described as being similar to an Ayrshire boll of meal, which means that it must have weighed around the equivalent of 6 bushels. At some point in history it is said that brawling soldiers broke the charter stone, and when the locals discovered this they made arrangements for the pieces to be built into the wall of the old church of St Nicholas, where it still remains.

In the town of Girvan there was at one time another sanctuary stone, originally located in High Street, which today is little more than a footpath connecting Hamilton Street with the Bridge Street car park. It was to this stone that mediaeval insolvent debtors were wont to flee in order to escape their creditors. Little else is known about this stone.

On the north side of the River Girvan, three miles from Girvan itself, is Killochan Castle, a particularly grand sixteenth century tower house, long owned by the Cathcart family but which has passed through a number of different owners in recent years. In a field to the west of the castle woodlands can be found the Baron's Stone of Killochan, a massive granite boulder. Geologically, this is a glacial erratic that was carried by ice from the Galloway Highlands around Loch Doon before being dumped here. The boulder, which has a relatively flat top, is reckoned to weigh 37 tons. The stone is thirteen yards in circumference. At one time the barons of Killochan estate met here to dispense justice.

A notable large stone is that known as Thougritstane, which lies in a field at Brandleside farm, north of Dunlop. The stone is celebrated in local legend, but there appears to be considerable doubt as to its real name. Thougritstane is how it is named on Ordnance Survey maps, both modern and old, and seems to be a local pronunciation of 'the

1.3 The Baron's Stone of Killochan, where the local laird used to execute malefactors. *(Dane Love)*

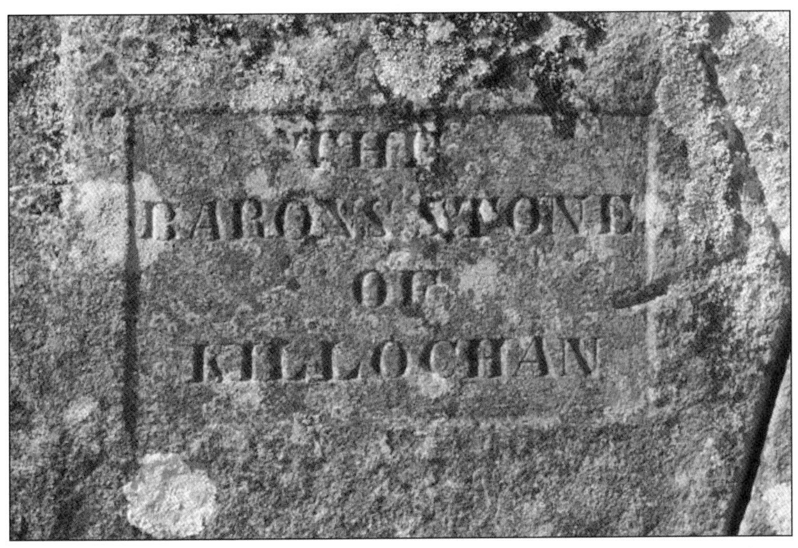

1.4 Detail of carved name on the Baron's Stone of Killochan. *(Dane Love)*

great stone'. However, delving into the local history of the parish we find it referred to as 'Ogirtstane' or 'Thugart Stane', and it is thought that these may derive from either the ogre's stone, the girth stone, or even Thor's great stone. Its etymology is no longer able to be fathomed.

As to the massive boulder, it is really a massive erratic, left on the slope of Brandleside Hill when the ice glaciers finally melted. Geologists have analysed the stone and discovered that it comprises of blue augitic porphyrite, and that the natural rock that lies under it different, proving that it was brought here by elements stronger than man. Its massive size in the middle of a grassy field has attracted the attentions of wonderers for centuries, and no doubt prehistoric man treated it as a place of worship. Rev Matthew Dickie mentioned the stone in the *New Statistical Account* in 1837, 'round which, if tradition is to be believed, it was customary for persons attending at the chapel [which lay to the east] to perform part of their devotions.' One of the possible derivations of the name may have associations with the local priest, for 'Tagairtstane' may derive from the Gaelic *an t-sagairt*, which means 'of the priest'.

Writing in *Ayrshire Nights' Entertainments*, published in 1894, John MacIntosh tells of a perhaps fanciful and certainly unrecorded legend associated with the stone. He claimed that even as recently as the time of the Reformation, Roman Catholics would have to do penance at the stone for various sins they had committed. They were sent to the stone, which at that time was located in an area where the ancient Chapel of St Mary existed, and had to crawl around the stone, shouting the mantra, 'O thou grit stane.' Some even said that the deity was present within the stone.

Thougritstane measures approximately twelve feet in length, by eight feet across, and an early surveyor, Robert Aitken, who visited in 1829, calculated it to weight 25 tons 8 hundredweight. The stone may have been associated with burials, for it was said that the farmer at Brandleside would not plough within a reasonable distance of the boulder, for fear of disturbing corpses. Indeed, the old tack or lease of the farm stipulated that the tenant should neither remove it nor cultivate its immediate vicinity. An early account of Dunlop parish, written by the local schoolmaster, J. D. Brown, claims that the stone may have at one time been a rocking stone, but that it lost its ability for movement with the build up of soil around it.

1.5 Thougritstane, which has many strange traditions associated with it.
(Dane Love)

Rocking stones are held in superstitious regard all over Scotland. Unfortunately, most of them have lost the ability to move over the centuries, and only the fading memory (or perhaps wishful thinking) of the locals confirm that these stones at one time were able to move gently when given a heavy push. The stones were dropped by melting glaciers, landing gently on their edges, and such was their equilibrium that they

1.6 The Rocking Stone on Cuff Hill, near Beith, is located in a circular wood.
(Dane Love)

could move. In Gaelic, the stones are known as *clach brach* or *clach-bhrath*, meaning, rocking stone, but they are otherwise known as logan stones, from the old English or Scots word 'log' meaning to rock.

In Ayrshire there are other former rocking stones at Loch Slochy, Cuff Hill and Lugar. The Loch Slochy stone is now difficult to find due to the close forestry plantations which grow around it. It is located in the Carrick Forest half a mile to the west of Loch Riecawr. However, the stone is of considerable size, and is perched on top of lesser boulders. Prior to the afforestation of the Galloway Highlands the stone would have been quite conspicuous on the moor, and almost due north of it, 150 yards away, stands another boulder, the Long Stone.

Cuff Hill is one of a group of small rounded hills located to the east of Beith. On the lower slopes of the hill are the remains of a chambered cairn, but near the summit, in a small round plantation surrounded by a drystone dike, can be found the Rocking Stone. Perched 633 feet

1.7 The Rocking Stone at Lugar, near Cumnock. *(Dane Love)*

above sea level, the Cuff Hill rocking stone was able to be rocked in 1842, according to the writer of the *New Statistical Account.* James Dobie of Crummock goes on to give some details of the stone itself.

'This stone is of common trap. Its specific gravity is 2.890; its figure an oblong spheroid; its contents 141 cubic feet; and weight 11 tons 7 cwts.' It is reckoned that the stone lost its ability to rock when some locals dug below it to ascertain its fulcrum. Local tradition maintains that this stone had druidical associations, the meaning of which have long since become obscure and forgotten.

The Rocking Stone at Lugar, east of Cumnock, is thought to be the remains of a burial chamber, and old accounts of it describe it as a 'dolmen' or 'cromlech'. It was also known as the Lamagee Stone in old accounts. It can be found in a small area of grass at the mouth of the Bello Path, a narrow rocky defile just before the Bello Water joins the Glenmuir Water to become the Lugar Water. It is not one of the biggest of rocking stones, being six feet long, five in height and three wide, but it has a small stone arc adjoining it. The stone is thought to have been able to rock until around 1800. As the stone has a number of other stones associated with it, it has been speculated that it was at one time part of a chambered cairn, but that the smaller stones were taken from it, leaving only the larger boulders that early man could not move.

The Witch's Stone, located near to the summit of the Craigs of Kyle, in the parish of Coylton, is said to have been another rocking stone. It

1.8 The Witch's Stone can be found on the summit of the Craigs of Kyle. *(Dane Love)*

stands proud from the surrounding landscape, and as such gained legends associating it with evil women. At one time there was a chapel on this hill top, dedicated to St Bride, all traces of which have long-since been removed. Whether or not the priest associated with the chapel thought that the rocking stone, with its eerie ability to move, despite its weight, was associated with witches or the devil is long forgotten. The stone is perched upon three others, and it has been calculated that the boulder weighs around thirty tons.

There is some dubiety concerning the Witch's Stone on the Craigs of Kyle. The Ordnance Survey, on maps from 1855 to the present, locate the stone further west, where a massive cuboidal block is perched near to the summit triangulation station. Not as large as the other boulder, this stone does have an extensive view, and on one side a small projection could be used as a seat.

On the opposite side of the Kerse valley from the Craigs of Kyle, on a low hill above Knockshinnoch farm, is the Carlin Knowe. Carlin is the old Scots word for a witch or old woman, and a prehistoric cairn occupies the top of the hillock. Another Carlin's Stone can be found on the summit of a small hillock to the east of Dunlop. Near to Craigends farm, which is located in the midst of forestry plantations to the east of Waterside, near Kilmarnock, can be found the Carlin Stane, perched next to the Carlin Burn.

Another rocking stone, known as the Logan Stone, can be found on the moors to the east of the Big Hill of Glenmount, on the west side of Loch Doon. This boulder, reported by John Smith in *Prehistoric Man in Ayrshire* in 1895, is located around a quarter of a mile to the west of the White Laise burial cairn, and around one mile south west of the dam. The stone is a granite boulder that has been deposited on the greywacke by the retreating ice flows that once covered the Galloway Highlands. It is said that it could easily be moved with the power of one hand. The stone measures four feet three inches in length by four feet wide and rises around three feet in height.

At Borestone farm, which lies southeast of Barrmill, in the parish of Beith, was a large boulder known as the Bore Stone. This is said to have been the gathering place of the men of the barony of Giffen, which comprised around half of the parish of Beith. It was long owned by the Montgomerie family, and Giffen Castle appears to have been the home of successive heirs to the Earls of Eglinton. The boulder had a rounded hole on its uppermost surface, and it was said that the laird, when he wished to raise his supporters, would place his flag on a flagstaff in the hole on the boulder. Being located on a reasonably prominent hill in the district, the followers would see the flag and be able to come out in support. In 1876 James Dobie recorded that the stone was around eleven and a half inches in diameter, comprised of sandstone. The stone was destroyed around 1950, Giffen Castle itself collapsing in the night of 12 April 1838.

Similarly, the Devil has been linked with a number of stones. The De'il Stone that existed at Cumnock can no longer be found on the ground, but reference to it is made in a number of old books. The stone was located by the banks of the Glaisnock Water, near to where the present road of Wyllie Crescent is. At one time this was open fields. The De'il Stone had a tradition associated with it that was common among the young folk of the district. It was said that if you ran round it three times then the devil himself would appear before you. The sandstone Glaisnock Viaduct that rises a few hundred yards upstream from where the boulder was located is sometimes referred to as the 'Deilstone Viaduct' in some accounts.

Another large boulder associated with the Devil can be seen near to Ladyland House, on the edge of the county, north of Kilbrinie. The De'il's Chuckie Stane is probably not a boulder as such, for it looks more to be like a protruding block of natural rock rather than a freestanding stone or rock. The name is of a humorous nature, a 'chuckie' being the Scots word for a small rounded pebble, and thus it is claimed that the Devil must be a giant figure, if this large rock is a mere pebble to him. The stone is located in a small stand of mature trees, within a few hundred yards of Ladyland House. On the surface of the rock are various fissures and grooves, probably striations created by flowing ice many millennia ago.

There are a few places in Ayrshire where some great event has been marked by the leaving of hand or foot prints in rocks or stones. One of these, which is mere legend yet commonly pointed out, is the hoof prints on the cobbles of the Auld Brig o' Doon, left by the grey mare of Tam o' Shanter on his escape from the witches. More of this will be found in the penultimate chapter, where we will look at some bridges

1.9 Wallace's Heel is a natural spring by the side of the River Ayr in Ayr itself, which was supposed to have been created by Sir William Wallace. *(Dane Love)*

with tales associated with them.

A similar story, however, is associated with a spot by the side of the River Ayr in Ayr itself. A path from Holmston Road leads down by the southern bank of the river, the path heading east towards the site of the Overmill. Not too far from Holmston Road, just before a small bridge over a tiny tributary of the river, a few steps lead down to the riverside. Here can be found a flat slab of natural rock, a few feet above the river level. By the side of the rock is a small spring, the water bubbling forth from a fissure in the slab. Affixed to the rock behind the spring is a small granite stone bearing the legend, *Wallace's Heel.*

The famous Scots freedom fighter, William Wallace, has a number of associations with Ayr, and this is one of the more significant, in that something tangible of his time remains to be seen. Wallace was in Ayr, but was being pursued by a number of English soldiers. He made his way eastwards, along the side of the River Ayr, heading for the remote wooded gorges of Auchincruive, where he expected to make his escape. A number of dogs were hot on his heels, the scent he had left behind being an easy indicator of the route he had taken. Wallace decided that in order to lose the dogs, he would jump into the River Ayr, wade upstream for a few hundred yards, then climb out onto the northern bank.

Just as he was making his way down the banking, the soldiers were catching up on him, so he jump down to the waterside and dived into the water. His final step on the southern bank of the river, on the flat sandstone slab, was of such force that his heel left its imprint in the rock. The Wallace managed to escape from his pursuers, and made his way to the fastnesses of Auchincruive. The rest, as some say, is history.

Wallace's Heel was a popular spot for tourists to visit in the Victorian period, when tales of Wallace's heroism and feats were gaining popularity, resulting in the erection of Wallace's Tower in Ayr, with its statue, and the Wallace Monument on Barnweill Hill, both in the county. Many a father took his son to the spot to show him the heel mark that was left by Wallace's boot, and often to take a drink from the spring. At one time a steel cup affixed to the rock by a chain was available for this purpose. On the opposite side of the river, in a steep bank, was a cavern known as Wallace's Cave, also said to have been a place where he hid from his pursuers. Little else is known about it.

The Granny Stane in Irvine has a number of legends and traditions associated with it. The stone is located in the middle of the River Irvine, almost directly below the Rivergate shopping centre. Previously, the stone was positioned on the upstream side of the original Irvine Bridge, which has crossed the river here for centuries. The stone was at one time more prominent in the watercourse, but the dam near to Burns' Statue was built in 1895 and the construction of the shopping centre has affected the level of the water, meaning that only the uppermost part of it is visible above the surface.

It is claimed that the Granny Stane was at one time part of a stone circle, perhaps the original place of worship in this area prior to the arrival of the Christian saints. The circle would have been located in the middle of an open plain, but over the centuries the River Irvine has changed its course a number of times, and some of the stones were washed away. It is also noted that in 1895 some of the remaining stones were removed by blasting, much against the will of many of the residents.

Some say that the Granny Stane is not named after some old

woman or witch, but that in fact the name derives from the Gaelic *grian*, meaning sun. This may be an allusion to the stone circle indicating winter and summer solstices, or else the circle was the place where the sun was worshipped.

Locally, a number of tales have become popular over the years concerning the stone. Some say that the stone was used as a stepping stone across the river, prior to the construction of the bridge. Other stones would have been located by its side, creating a perilous crossing of the river. It was claimed that William Wallace came this way prior to an attack on the English soldiers. Others claim that at one time the carters, who used to transport coal and other goods from the harbour to the town, used to circle the stone in order to bring good luck.

1.10 The old stone at Fairlie is now to be seen in the church. *(Dane Love)*

At Fairlie, on the coast south of Largs, can be seen an old stone that has become legendary in the village for its historical associations. Some know it as the Old Man of Fairlie, but this is a fairly recent appellation that has been applied to the stone, for old accounts do not seem to give it a name. The stone is now inset in the wall of the vestibule of Fairlie Parish Church. On its can be seen carvings of a human figure and two animals.

The story of the stone has been traced back to an old chapel that seems to have stood somewhere by the side of the little Keppen Burn, which tumbles steeply from the Whatside Hills, between Fairlie and Kelburn. Little is known about the chapel, but at some point its stones were removed to allow the erection of a shepherd's cottage, which was given the name Chapelhouse. An old well, perhaps associated with the chapel, is known to have existed alongside. The cottage of Chapelhouse has at least one story associated with it. John, 3rd Earl of Glasgow, was fighting at the Battle of Fontenoy in 1745 but he received wounds and was unable to walk. A fellow soldier, who belonged to Kilbirnie, found him and carried him back to safety. Accordingly, Lord Glasgow arranged for the cottage at Chapelhouse to be restored and it was given to his rescuer rent free for the remainder of his life.

In 1844, James, 5th Earl of Glasgow, had Chapelhouse demolished, and he allowed the newly-established Free Church congregation in Fairlie to take the stone and use them in the erection of a manse in the village. When the cottage was demolished, the carved stone, which measures four feet three inches by fifteen inches wide, and which had formed the lintel over the fireplace, was saved and kept separate from the rest of the stones. The Free Church minister, Rev Gemmell, had the stone erected in the manse garden, where it remained for many years.

The stone has been dated to around the ninth or tenth centuries, the carvings being similar in style to those on the Inchinnan Cross. The man is lying prostrate, perhaps holding a round shield and a sword, though these are much worn. The central beast has its mouth open, facing the man, as though it is ready to eat him. The animal on the right has its head turned back, its tail held in its own mouth.

CHAPTER TWO

CAVES and GROTTOES

There are a number of caves across the Ayrshire countryside that have legends or tales associated with them. Some of these caves have known historical associations, and a few will be mentioned in this chapter.

One of the more famous accounts associated with a cave is that of the cannibal Sawney Bean. Much has been written about this over the years, and the present account can add no more than what has been related previously. It is said that Sawney Bean and his family established themselves in a cave to the south of Lendalfoot, along the Carrick shore.

2.1 Sawney Bean's Cave is to be found in the headland at the northern end of Balcreuchan Port. *(Dane Love)*

There are no historical references to Sawney Bean, nor any other cannibal, in the historical records of Ayrshire, but his story is one that has persisted. The tale has been used by a number of writers over the centuries, most notably by S. R. Crockett, who used the tale in his novel, *The Grey Man*, written in 1896, and still available. The earliest reference to the story of Sawney Bean appears to have been written in a broadsheet of around 1700. Perhaps the account that made the story more popular was that in John Nicholson's *Historical and Traditional Tales connected with the South of Scotland*, published in 1843, until Crockett's novel appeared.

Sawney Bean's cave can be found on the shore below the A77, at a narrow bay known as Balcreuchan Port. A steep path from a car park adjacent to the road drops down to the stony beach, where the waves usually batter against the land, throwing up stones and debris. At the north end of this cove, where the headland juts into the sea, a narrow cave is pointed out as being the one in which the cannibal family were supposed to have lived. Access to the cave is possible when the sea is calm enough and the tide is low. Torches should be taken in order to view the interior, but the reader will appreciate that this cave is probably too narrow in order to allow a family to live within it in any form of comfort, never mind the dampness. Some accounts claim that the original cave penetrated the cliff-side for up to one mile, but other accounts, which are more realistic, state that the cave is seventy feet deep.

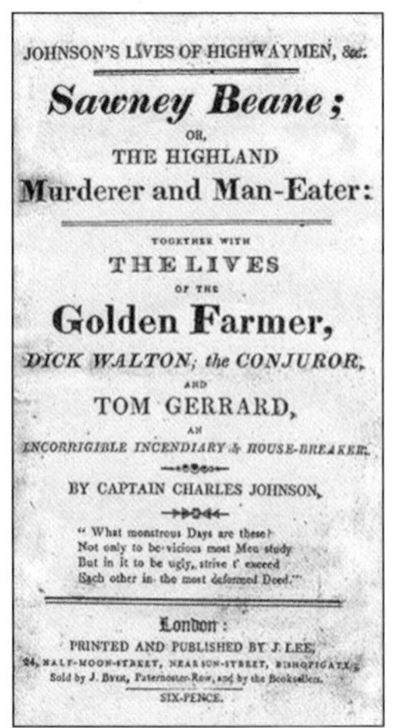

JOHNSON'S LIVES OF HIGHWAYMEN, &c.

Sawney Beane;

OR,

THE HIGHLAND

Murderer and Man-Eater:

TOGETHER WITH

THE LIVES

OF THE

Golden Farmer,

DICK WALTON; the CONJUROR,

AND

TOM GERRARD,

AN

INCORRIGIBLE INCENDIARY & HOUSE-BREAKER.

BY CAPTAIN CHARLES JOHNSON.

"What monstrous Days are these?
Not only to be vicious most Men study
But in it to be ugly, strive t' exceed
Each other in the most deformed Deed."

London:

PRINTED AND PUBLISHED BY J. LEE,
24, HALF-MOON-STREET, NEAR SUN-STREET, BISHOPSGATE;
Sold by J. Bysh, Paternoster-Row, and by the Booksellers.

SIX-PENCE.

2.2 The story of Sawney Bean has existed for many years, and has been told in various early chapbooks. *(Author's Collection)*

According to Rev Charles Hill Dick, writing in *Highways and Byways in Galloway and Carrick*, first published in 1916, Sawney Bean's Cave was at that time used by gypsies and other tramps at night as a place of refuge.

The traditional tale, however, takes us back to the reign of King James – whether James I of Scotland or James VI of Scotland and I of England is never really established.

In any case, at that time the route between Girvan and Stranraer was a remote location, the roadway being little more than a rough track up and down the cliffs. Ballantrae had not been established as a village yet, so there were few settlements in the district other than a few clachans or ferm-touns. Over the years one or two travellers seemed to become lost on this route, and to start with folk put this down to them falling over the cliffs to their death in the sea. However, one day a couple of travellers were making their way over Bennane Head when they were ambushed by a wild bunch of hairy men and women.

The attackers spoke no English, speaking to each other in grunts and growls. One of the travellers was killed and dragged from their horse, but the other got away and managed to raise the alarm. When it was known that there were highway robbers on this stretch of trackway, the locals put two and two together and realised that many of those who had disappeared over the years had probably also been killed. Accordingly, a party of soldiers were sent from Edinburgh to track down the miscreants.

At first nothing could be found of the robbers, but eventually a faint pathway was spotted heading towards the cliffs. The route was followed, and tracking dogs soon sniffed out the cave. Armed with guns and swords, the soldiers made their way inside, only to discover a whole family living within. What they did not expect to see, however, were dead human bodies and skeletons, the remains of those murdered and robbed by the roadside. The cave family had been taking the bodies and cutting bits from them. These were then cooked and used to feed the cannibal family. The soldiers managed to round up what was little more than a group of wild savages and escort them to Edinburgh where they were executed.

Sawney Bean is often said to have been a man named Alexander MacBean, or Beane, who was originally a hedger or ditcher from East Lothian. For some reason he made his way to Galloway and Carrick and settled there. He took a common-law-wife, known as Black Agnes Douglas, who some say was banished from Ballantrae for being a witch. Together they produced many children, 46 of which were arrested when the cave was raided.

The tale of Sawney Bean is one of long-standing, though it is not only to be found in southern Ayrshire. It has also been retold in

Galloway, the cave being located along the Solway shores. Other places have related similar tales and, of course, trawls through the official records have never produced any evidence of the existence of the cannibals.

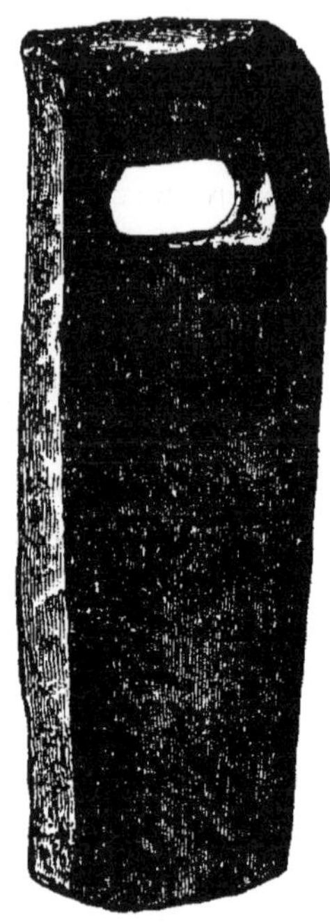

2.3 A bone object found in the Holy Cave at Hunterston during early excavations. *(Author's Collection)*

On the coast between Hunterston Power Station and Portencross Castle, at the foot of the steep cliffs that make up the Hawking Craig and the Three Sisters, is an ancient cave. Known as the Holy Cave, the earliest traditional associations with it date from the time when St Kentigern or Mungo, the patron saint of Glasgow, lived, which was approximately *c.*520-*c.*612. The saint was the son of Thenew or Enoch, a daughter of a king of Lothian, and was born at Culross in Fife. Following an education by St Serf, he spent some of his time in Glasgow, using this cave as a retreat, where he could hide from the public and spend time in contemplation.

The cave was measured as being 27 feet deep, the average width and height being around six feet. The entrance is wide and open, but soon it contracts to a recess measuring nine feet long, four feet wide and six feet high. In the late nineteenth century the cave mouth was excavated and old pottery, ashes, bones and other items were discovered, indicating a long period of occupation.

Within the cave can be found a deep well, a rather dangerous place for visitors today. In later years this well was reputed to have curative powers, and many pilgrims suffering from various ailments would make their way there in search of a cure. Known as the Wishing Well, Rev John Lamb in 1896 claims that this name derives from the Saxon *visa-an*, which means 'wiseman' or 'philosopher', and that the name actually means 'The Instructor's Well'. This is perhaps rather fanciful, the cleric being against the thought of his parishioners making their way to the well and throwing coins into it, making wishes and hoping that some unseen spirit would help to bring them true. He goes on to relate that the cave was resorted to on the first Sunday in May, the pilgrims drinking the water in the hope of a cure for a variety of ailments. At other times, people went to the well with the minister and had their children baptised in the waters.

In a number of locations across the county, where the natural rock is the bright red sandstone associated with Mauchline and Ballochmyle, or some other soft stone, a number of caves have been made by man for a variety of purposes. Some of these are purely fanciful but have gained tales or stories associated with them over the intervening years.

Within Barskimming estate, near Mauchline, are a number of caves and tunnels carved in the solid rock. Barskimming House stands on the south side of the River Ayr, perched high on a cliff above the river, whereas the stable block is located on the opposite side. Between the two is what is known as Barskimming New Bridge, in fact an old bridge of 1788. In the cliff below the bridge is a building perched in a shelf, carved out of the solid sandstone. Near Barskimming is a tunnel through the rock, reaching a ledge and windows from where a view of the river below can be had. Another cave is located n the north side of the river, at the head of Netheraird Holm. Further downstream, but still on the estate, a cave has been carved out of the sandstone below Burnfoot Lodge. This seems to have been used as a stable, for within it was a place for a horse, and a fireplace for the stable-lad. The fireplace had its own chimney carved through the rock and joining the chimney of the cottage above.

On Auchinleck estate the Lugar Water and Dippol Burn have carved their way through the soft sandstone, creating deep gorges with near vertical, and in some cases overhanging, cliffs. There are two man-made caves or grottoes near to the present Auchinleck House, one of which has gained the reputation of being used by Sir William Wallace.

Just downstream from where the Dippol Burn passes from the steep gorge into the Lugar Water, on the north side of the water, can be seen what has been called Wallace's Cave. This comprises one rock-cut compartment, measuring approximately fourteen feet wide by twelve feet deep. The roof is around ten feet in height in the centre. The entrance doorway is lancet-shaped, around seven feet in height. To its

2.4 Wallace's Cave is located within a dangerous cliff in Auchinleck estate. *(Dane Love)*

left, when seen from the outside, is a small pointed window. Inside, the floor is perfectly flat, as are the side walls. In the four corners are large rounded ribs, rising up the corners of the room and curving over on the ceiling to form a cross, or perhaps a saltire.

Wallace's Cave is something of an enigma. Dating it has proved to be difficult – some historians assume that it was formed in the late thirteenth or early fourteenth century, and that Wallace did in fact use

2.5 The interior of Wallace's Cave, which has been carved from the solid rock. *(Dane Love)*

it to hide. Others claim that it was merely carved out in the eighteenth century by the Boswell owners of the estate. Perhaps at the time there was a surge in interest in Wallace, much as the recent film *Braveheart* did in the late twentieth century, and the Boswells decided to create their own folly and name it after Wallace.

It's not as if there is no connection with Wallace and Auchinleck. At the time Wallace was fighting for the freedom of Scotland from England, he was accompanied by Nicol de Auchinleck, owner of Auchinleck estate and castle at that time. The Auchinleck Castle that he would have lived in is the first of the three successive homes on the estate. The second castle, or Old Place of Auchinleck, stands in ruins to the east, and the third home, the present Auchinleck House, dates from 1754 and is currently owned by the Landmark Trust. 'Blind' Harry the Minstrel, who wrote the epic poem *The Acts and Deeds of Sir William Wallace* around 1508, makes reference to Auchinleck's part in the campaign for independence.

Nicol Auchinleck of that Ilk was Wallace's uncle, according to some. He took part in an attack on Glasgow Castle around 1300, leading 140 men up the city's Drygait to join Wallace in his battle with the foe.

Auchinleck's men attacked from the rear, leaving the English in a state of confusion. This allowed Wallace to rush forward and split Earl Percy's head in two halves with a single stroke of his mighty broadsword. Thus ended the Battle of the Bell of the Brae. The English men then fled up Clydesdale to Bothwell where they were able to regroup. Blind Harry's version tells us:

> Auchinleck said, 'We shall do all we may,
> We would like ill to bide ought lang away;
> A boutteous ttail betwixt us soon must be,
> But to the right Almighty God have eye.'
> Adam Wallace and Auchinleck were bown,
> Sevenscore with them on the back-side of the town;
> Right fast they yeed, while they were out of sight,
> The other part arrayed them full right.
>
> Adam Wallace and Auchinleck came in,
> And parted Southeron right suddenly in twin,
> Return'd to them as noble men in wear,
> The Scots got room, and many down they bear.

Access to Wallace's Cave is extremely difficult, for the Dippol Burn, which can often run in spate, is awkward to cross and on the opposite side the pathway to the cave doorway can be slippery. At one point the path to the cave has steps cut from the rock, hinting that the cave was in fact constructed as a folly, to which genteel ladies and gentlemen from the 'big house' would walk before dinner.

A second cave in the grounds of the house is to be found in the rocks by the side of the Dippol Burn. Known as the Deer Cave, this cavern is known to have been carved from the rock in the eighteenth century, for Dr Samuel Johnson, friend of James Boswell, made reference to it in his *A Journey to the Western Islands of Scotland*, written in 1774:

> At no great distance from the house runs a pleasing brook, by a red rock, out of which has been hewn a very agreeable and commodious summer-house, at less expence, as Lord

Auchinleck told me, than would have been required to build a room of the same dimensions. The rock seems to have no more dampness than any other wall. Such opportunities of variety it is judicious not to neglect.

2.6 The Deer Cave on Auchinleck estate was carved from the sandstone by Lord Auchinleck. *(Dane Love)*

Within, the cave is semi-circular, measuring around fifteen feet diameter. It rises around ten feet in height. The walls of the cave have what appear to be cornices around the wallheads, creating what was the fashionable style at the time for room decoration. Over this are sloping cornices, all carved from the solid sandstone. The doorway and windows have gothic tops to them, and at one time had frames and glazing.

Just a few hundred yards downstream from the Deer Cave, or Summer House, as it was also known, can be found the old ice house associated with Auchinleck House. Like the two caves on the estate, this has been carved from the solid rock, the small doorway giving access to a large egg-shaped container, at one time used for storing meat and other foodstuffs that had to be kept frozen.

There are a number of other caves across Ayrshire that have been associated with William Wallace. To the south of Alloway, on the high road to Maybole, the road crosses the Long Glen by means of what is known as the Halfway Bridge, being midway between Ayr and Maybole. Downstream from the bridge, in the wooded glen and below the small waterfall that tumbles over the rocks, was a cavern shown on old maps as 'Wallace's Cave'. Although there is no evidence that Wallace actually hid here, local tradition claims that he did.

Less than half a mile from Wallace's Cave in the Long Glen is an ancient boulder known as Wallace's Stone. Although not well known, more people are aware of this ancient relic than of the cave. The boulder is surrounded by a low drystone dike, just off the roadway into Blairston Mains farm. Measuring about six feet by three feet, the granite boulder rises around two feet off the ground. Old stories claim that Wallace rested here prior to making an entry into Ayr. As he waited, he lay his claymore down on the boulder and, rather fancifully in some accounts, the shape of it was miraculously left behind. Others claim that the shape of the sword was drawn round by Wallace's supporters, and was later chiselled into the rock.

In any case, the boulder has what some claim to be the image of Wallace's sword carved upon it. This is around three and a half feet in

2.7 Wallace's Stone at Blairston Mains, south of Ayr, has a cross carved on it that may represent the patriot's sword. *(Dane Love)*

length, and the hilt is around fourteen inches across. The end of the shaft opposite the crosshead is pointed in appearance, a fact that may have suggested a sword to some observers.

The boulder, even to supporters of the Wallace theory, is obviously an ancient stone cross, the 'sword' being in fact a Christian cross, the head of which is like a Maltese cross is style. It is thought to date from the tenth to twelfth century. As such, the stone probably predates Wallace's time by almost four centuries, having been erected by the early Christians in the area. It has been speculated that the stone, which would have been positioned upright, marked one of the early pilgrim routes to Whithorn.

2.8 Statue of Sir William Wallace on the site of the old tolbooth in Ayr. *(Dane Love)*

The present location of Wallace's Stone is not its original. Prior to being located by the side of the road into Blairston Mains, the stone was actually located at the Long Glen, near to Wallace's Cave. This may explain the supposed connection with Wallace. At some time the stone was moved, it being said that six Clydesdale horses were required to drag it. It had been proposed taking it to a more prominent position, and upending it, but the stone proved to be too difficult to manoeuvre and it was left recumbent, a low stone wall erected around it.

A different tradition concerning this stone was recorded by Sir William Abercrummie in 1696. He noted that the cross was alleged to have been made by a venerable churchman who had mediated a peace between the King of the Picts and the King of the Scots. Abercrummie also related the Wallace legend, giving two variations – the sword shape was miraculously left behind whilst Wallace slept, or that the incision was made by Wallace's sword whilst he fought the English at this place.

At the time of the Covenanters, which was between 1638 and 1688, the Presbyterians of south-west Scotland were forced to flee from their homes and hide in the wilds of the surrounding countryside. The king and government were trying to force Episcopacy on the Scots, but the Covenanters resisted this, often with many fatal consequences. There are few parish kirkyards in much of Ayrshire that do not have at least one Covenanting martyr buried within them. Forced to live rough, many Covenanters found caves in which to shelter, and a number of locations across the county are known to have been used for this purpose.

By the side of the Dunton Water, in the parish of Fenwick, can be found Dunton Cove. This cavern is located half-way up a steep rock face, and looks north over the river to the moors of Dick's Law and the Flow Moss. Many of the local farms and shepherds' houses were occupied by Covenanters and in times of difficulty many of them flocked to this cave for safety. Although today the cave appears to be quite open, at the time of the Covenanters there were more bushes around, and one of these was cut down and hauled up to the entrance, camouflaging it from passing soldiers. The size of the cavern, which appears to be natural, was large enough to conceal around half a dozen men.

A story is told of some Covenanters being pursued by the

dragoons. They ran as fast as they could across the moors towards the cave. Scrambling up the rock face they were able to enter the cave and lie low at the back of the hollow. The soldiers, who were following at some distance, did not want to get wet crossing the water, but had seen the Covenanters making their way into the cave. From the opposite bank of the river they fired their guns into the mouth of the cave. After a number of bullets had been spent, they left, thinking that the cave had become the grave of its occupants. However, as the Covenanters had all been lying on the floor the bullets had missed their targets.

2.9 Peden's Cave is located by the side of the Lugar Water, near to Ochiltree, and was a hiding place of Rev Alexander Peden, the famous Covenanting minister. *(SCMA Collection)*

Rev Alexander Peden, one of the more famous Covenanting ministers, used a number of caves across the county to hide from the soldiers who were searching for him. One of the caves he hid in can be found by the side of the Lugar Water, north-west of the village of Ochiltree. Accessed from near Auchinbay farm, the cave is actually a large hollow in a sandstone rock that rises on the south side of the river. Access to the cave is made down a few roughly-hewn steps, and here the famous preacher hid on a number of occasions. He was perhaps in hiding here during the last few days of his life, for he was to make his way to his brother's farm at Tenshillingside, on Auchinleck estate, where he died on 26 January 1686. He was secretly buried in the kirkyard at Auchinleck, but the soldiers discovered this and a few weeks later dug up his body and carted it off to Cumnock, where he was buried at the foot of the gallows tree. A white granite monument erected in 1891 marks his grave.

A second Peden's Cave in Ayrshire is to be found on Craigie Hill, to the south of Kilmarnock. Just two fields away from the village of Craigie, the cave is located in a field on the northern slopes of one of the rough hillocks that form the hilltop. This 'cave' is not really one, for it comprises of two large boulders, lying at an angle and creating a place of shelter. Peden preached a service at this place in October 1665.

A third Peden's Cave is located in the southern part of the county, in the hill pass known as the Nick of the Balloch. There, by the roadside, which in Covenanting times would be little more than a drovers' track, was a cave said to have been used by the wandering preacher. That he was in this district is confirmed by the other hideout, Peden's Hut, shown on the maps above the Water of Girvan, between Loch Skelloch and the Cornish Loch. Further east, in Loch Riecawr, was Peden's Isle, now much submerged by the construction of the dam.

2.10 On the side of Craigie Hill, south of Kilmarnock, Rev Alexander Peden also hid between two boulders which formed another Peden's Cave. *(Dane Love)*

Other caves associated with the Covenanters include Benan's Cave, which was located on the hillside above Old Dailly, east of Girvan. The Dalreoch Cave was to be found on the hillside on the south side of the River Stinchar from Colmonell. Situated above Dalreoch House, the cave has probably been destroyed by quarrying that took place in the immediate vicinity.

One of the more famous Covenanters' caves was known as the Aughty of the Star. This appears to have been located somewhere in the midst of the Galloway highlands, around Loch Enoch or Loch Macaterick. No known location for the cave can be found today, and it is possible that the cave was a man-made hideout, similar to what Bonnie Prince Charlie's Cage, or Cave, on the west side of Loch Ericht was like. The cave was a frequent haunt of the persecuted Covenanters, but it became well known to readers of literature, being mentioned in S. R. Crockett's novel, *The Raiders*, published in 1894. There he describes the cave:

> 'This,' said Silver Sand, 'is the Aughty of the Star. Ye have heard o' it, but few have seen it since the Killing Time. It is the best hiding-place in all broad Scotland.'
>
> I looked about at the famous cave which had sheltered nearly all the wanderers, from Cargill to Renwick – which had been safe haven in many a storm, for which both Clavers and Lag sought in vain. My father told me also how he and Patrick Walker the pedlar (he that scribes the stories of the sufferers and has them printed), went to seek for the Aughty; but, though Patrick Walker had lain in it for four nights in the days of the Highland Host, he could never find it again.

In Crockett's *The Men of the Moss Hags*, published in 1898, the hero hides in a cave in the same vicinity, styled 'Cove Macaterick' in the novel. This may, in fact, be the same cavern.

At Lugar, east of Cumnock, can be found Murdoch's Cave, which is located below the mill house associated with Bello Mill. It is named after William Murdoch (1754-1839), the famous inventor who worked with Boulton and Watt. He invented gas lighting, which was his most notable discovery, but he also made a number of improvements and additions to the steam engine, and may also be able to stake a claim as the person who made the first self-propelled vehicle, for he added wheels to a steam engine and allowed it to drive along a road. Murdoch is said to have carried out his early experiments with coal gas in the cave below the mill house, a square cavern hewn from the rock. The cave has little more than a door and a narrow window. A plaque commemorating Murdoch is affixed to the house at Bello Mill.

The smugglers who haunted much of Ayrshire in the eighteenth and other centuries used a number of caves whilst they transported their contraband into and across the county. Smugglers are usually associated with the coast, but in fact they had to transport their goods across country to the markets in places like Glasgow. A cave near to Ladyland House, north of Kilbirnie, is known as the Smugglers' Cave from its use at the time. Located by the side of the Maich Water, next to a waterfall in a steep gorge, the cave was at one time reached through an entrance that had sandstone pillars guarding it. The associations with smugglers may be little more than a tale, and in fact the cave may just be a folly within the ornamental policies that surround Ladyland House. The Ordnance Survey Six Inch map of 1855 does not show the cave, but it does indicate a footpath that wanders through the woods by the side of the Maich Water, past the various waterfalls, no doubt a short but pleasant stroll for the occupants of Ladyland either before or after dinner.

Another Smugglers' Cave can be seen in the grounds of Kelburn Castle, south of Largs. A path from the castle makes its way up the side of the Kel Burn and soon arrives at a waterfall of some considerable size. The cave is located nearby.

Probably one of the most famous smugglers' caves can be found under Culzean Castle, on the rocky Carrick shore. The ancient name for the castle that stood on the headland above these caverns is Coif, or Cove, which is the old Scots version of cave. It was not until the eighteenth century that the name was changed to Culzean, to tie in with the laird's title. In the cliffs under the castle, facing the waters of the firth, are six caverns of various sizes. The *Statistical Account* of 1792 gives a fairly detailed account of the size of these caves:

> Of the three towards the west, the largest has its entry as low as high water mark, the roof is about 50 feet high; and has the appearance as if two large rocks had fallen together, forming a Gothic arch, though very irregular; it extends inwards about 200 feet, and varies in breadth. It communicates with the other two, which are both considerably less, but of much the same irregular form. Towards the east are the other three coves, which likewise

communicate with each other. They are nearly of the same height and figure with the former, but their extent has not been precisely ascertained. Whether these coves are natural or artificial, and if artificial, what has been their design, no tradition whatever informs us. One circumstance, however, cannot be omitted. To the largest of the three west-most coves, is a door or entry, built of free-stone, with a window three feet above the door, of the same kind of work; above both these, there is an apartment, from which might be sent down whatever could annoy the assailants at the door. The last circumstance is well known to take place in many of the old castles in the country, and seems to indicate, that at least this part of the coves has been at one period or another, the abode of some of the inhabitants of this country.

2.11 Underneath Culzean Castle, facing the sea, are a number of caves and tunnels that were used when smuggling was rife along the Carrick shore. *(Dane Love)*

Culzean was for centuries a seat of the Kennedy family, until it was passed by them to the National Trust for Scotland. In the early eighteenth century the castle was home to Sir John Kennedy, who was known to be a smuggler of some standing. As well as legitimate imports, he also ran goods to Scotland from the Isle of Man and other locations. In 1726 a boat in which he had a joint share sank in the Firth of Clyde, losing its cargo of barley, much used in the manufacture of whisky. Again, on another occasion, one of his boats was seized en route from the Isle of Man with contraband goods on board worth £344. The Kennedys were able to land their illicit goods in Culzean Bay, where a stretch of sand and shingle hidden from view forms the beach to the north of the castle, and quickly get it hidden under lock and key in the caves.

The following is a true story of a smuggling wherry that landed on Culzean shore in February 1777. The boat had become grounded when a revenue cutter, manned by the excise men, came upon it. The smugglers fired at the cutter, and one of the excise men was injured. The five smugglers were captured, and their contraband confiscated. However, when the contraband was being transferred to the authorities, it was discovered that much of it had disappeared, stolen by the excise men. Their leader, David Reid, wanted the crew dismissed from the revenue service, but soon found that they were only paid sixpence per day and had to turn out for service at a moment's notice. They were basically taking the goods to sell in order to earn a decent wage. The five smugglers were locked up in the tolbooth, but within days they had escaped, no doubt assisted by the gaoler who was sympathetic to their cause.

At one time the caves at Culzean were linked with the castle itself, but over the years the route has become blocked. This probably took place in the later eighteenth century when the present large castle was erected by Robert Adam. At that time Adam had to erect a large pillar in the centre of the cave to support the foundations of the castle, built on the headland above. The caves were partially excavated in 2003, as part of the television programme *Extreme Archaeology*, and in the floor were found remnants of old glass bottles, used to carry brandy and other spirits. Also found were hundreds of butchered mammal bones, as well as several human bones.

CHAPTER THREE

WELLS and WATER

There are a number of ancient wells in Ayrshire that have been celebrated in history or legend for various reasons. Some of these were assumed to contain curative waters, and should this be drunk then the patient would soon recover from whatever ailment the well was traditionally supposed to cure. Other wells were seen as being places of pilgrimage, dedicated to various saints, and even more were just celebrated in tradition for other reasons.

Probably the well with the longest association of having curative powers is Kingcase, or Bruce's Well, which lies between Prestwick and Ayr. Today it is located on a grassy area, just off Prestwick Road, in Maryborough Road. The well mouth is situated down a few steps, built up with stone walls. Surrounded by stone paving, the well is now protected by iron railings. At one end is a small drinking bowl.

The well is known to be an ancient one, and at some time its waters were recognised as having curative powers. King Robert the Bruce is supposed to have been hunting in the shire when he came to the well. The king is known to have suffered from a skin complaint, often described as leprosy, and it is said that he washed his broken skin in the waters. For some time after, the Bruce's skin improved, and he was to recognise the part played by the well by founding a 'spital', or leper house here. If the spital was already in existence by the time of Bruce's visit, it is thought that he further endowed it. Old charters from the king's son, Robert II, confirm that the lands of Spittalshiels (now Shields) and Robertlone (now Loans) in the locality were granted to the keepers of the well. Each year, the farmers of Colennan and Crossburn, in the parish of Dundonald, had to contribute to the spital.

In later years, when the spital had disappeared, this donation was still paid by the farmers, for example, in the early 1900s the tenant of Crossburn paid 56 bolls of meal and 28 merks as his contribution, now paid to Ayr Poorhouse. Apparently, the Duke of Portland refunded the cost of the meal to whoever was his tenant at the time.

There are some less likely traditions associating Bruce with the well. One of these claims that he was in the area hunting but was feeling tired. He lay down at this spot, sticking his spear into the ground as he slept. Once he had rested, the Bruce stood up and pulled his spear from the ground. Miraculously, the waters started to flow from the ground, creating a new spring. Bruce washed his face in the new fountain, and when the water helped his leprosy, he established the lazar colony here.

In 1911 the Bruce's Well was taken over by Prestwick Burgh and it was restored the following year. The well underwent further restoration work in 1963. The remains of St Ninian's Hospital stand nearby, forming a U-shaped section of walling.

Drinking water from mineral wells does not seem to have been as popular in Ayrshire as it was in other parts of the country. A number of wells and springs were noted in various early accounts of the county as having mineral qualities, and it was reported that some people resorted to these in order to take the waters in the hope of a cure for some ailment or other. Few mineral wells were developed beyond clearing out the opening and perhaps adding a wall behind it.

One of the few mineral wells that were developed in a bigger scale was that at Saltcoats. The mineral well, or 'Pheesic', from physic well, was located within the Holm Wood, a plantation that was positioned north of the railway at South Beach Station. Situated by the side of the Stanley Burn, just off Caledonia Road, in the nineteenth century the well had a well house erected over it. This was a single storey structure, in size little more than a modern garage, but it had a small window on the rear elevation and two on the front, with lattice windows. A projecting porch protected the entrance door, over which a sign proclaimed 'Mineral Well'. Built of stone, with quoins at the corners, the well house had a slate roof and on both gables were chimney stacks.

Locals, as well as visitors to Saltcoats and Ardrossan, used to make their way to the well to sample the water. A number of summer seats were located around the building, it being a popular halt on walks. In

3.1 Water from the mineral well at Saltcoats was in demand as a cure for rheumatism. *(Author's Collection)*

the well house a glass of the water could be purchased for one penny. It was said that the water was a suitable cure for indigestion and rheumatism, as well as other ailments. On certain times of the year fetes were held in the vicinity of the well house, and these attracted many people. An old picture of 1910 shows a busy fete day at the well. Some of the water from Saltcoats' well was taken away and carbonated and put into bottles for sale. One Glasgow chemist apparently analysed the contents of the water and confirmed that it did have some health-giving properties. By the time of the Second World War the attraction of mineral springs had waned, and once the war was over they basically lost all of their attraction. The well house at Saltcoats was demolished and the well lost.

In West Kilbride the Toddy Well had a reputation amongst the villagers for having properties that could cure many ailments. The well, which was located in Kirktonhall Glen, had existed for many years, and was resorted to 'with a view to obtaining a supply of water supposed to be peculiarly adapted to the making of a beverage which so many think to be a cure for all human ills and woes.' Thus wrote a devout man of the cloth, Rev John Lamb, in 1896, who probably failed to mention that one of the principal ingredients of a toddy was whisky!

Another ancient curative well was located near to Pennyglen farm, on the road between Maybole and Culzean. This well contained waters with curative powers for cattle. Should any cow be suffering from what the farmers referred to as 'mure-ill', if they were given a drink from this well then their health began to improve, and they usually made a full recovery. So successful was the water from this well that farmers came from far and wide to fill bottles of water, which was taken back to cure individual cows or herds of cattle. Writing in 1696, Rev William Abercrummie noted that by that time the spring was quite neglected.

3.2 The Salt Well at the Bloak, west of Stewarton, had a well-house built over it. *(Dane Love)*

The Bloak Well near Stewarton was first discovered when pigeons were wont to flock around it around 1810. The well, which is in fact a chalybeate spring, was discovered to have waters of an iron-bearing nature, soon recognised for its medicinal quality. The well, although nowhere near as popular as the spa towns, was important enough for the local landowner, William Cuninghame of Lainshaw (1776-1849), to erect a well-house over it in 1833. He also appointed a well-keeper to look after the waters, and to supply them to those in need. The well-house survives, a simple white-painted cottage sitting by the roadside, now known as Salt Well. Fairly undistinguished at first glance, the cottage does have a carved cornice along the top of the front wall, marking it as more important that the more usual vernacular cottage. The well can no longer be seen, for it is believed to be located below the floor of the kitchen in the present cottage.

William Cunninghame seems to have been a keen supporter of mineral wells, for on his immediate estate, a few hundred yards north-west of Lainshaw House, which still stands to the west of Stewarton, is a chalybeate spring. The waters from this source were known to have curative powers, and an early account claims that they were restorative in curing 'the colic, the melancholy, and the vapours; it made the lean fat, the fat lean; it killed flat worms in the belly, loosened the clammy humours of the body, and dried the over-moist brain.' A number of bore-holes were sunk in the immediate vicinity, and the waters were used to supply agricultural troughs, being beneficial to the cattle. Today the spring has been covered over, though the waters still gurgle from the earth, being piped into the nearby Chapel Burn, for which the spring is the source.

At the time when the *Old Statistical Account* was written, around 1790-4 in the case of Ayrshire, the fascination of chalybeate and other mineral wells was still popular. Many parish accounts make reference to wells in the district that had iron or minerals within them, and often it was hoped that these would result in incoming commerce on the scale of Moffat well, or Strathpeffer, if not that of Bath! In the parish of Barr, remotely located on the moors almost midway between the villages of Barrhill and Barr itself, at that time around three or four miles from the nearest road, was a well known as the Shalloch Well. Today this is a remote cottage hidden in the depths of the Carrick Forest. Rev Stephen Young, minister of Barr when the *Account* was written, notes with possibility that there were many mineral wells in the parish, and that this one was pre-eminent at the time. 'The virtues of the water are well known in this country; it is a pretty strong chalybeate, and partakes of the sulphur also to no inconsiderable degree. About thirty years ago [that is, around 1760], people of the first rank and fashion in Carrick and the neighbourhood, attended this well; but this is not the case at present; every season, however, produces some company, and the waters have been rarely known to fail in giving relief to persons afflicted with

3.3 Kilwinning Abbey monks played a trick on the locals by causing blood to flow from the well there. *(Author's Collection)*

stomachic or scorbutic disorders. The reason why this water is in a great measure deserted, is the want of proper accommodation at the well,' in addition to the difficulty of access!

A spring that existed on the estate of Barbieston, now part of Skeldon estate, at Dalrymple, was at one time a popular spot for locals to take the waters. Known as the Physic Well, the spring was located by the side of the River Doon, at the foot of the steep banking where the Doon makes a sharp turn to the left, below Skeldon drive. The spring was known to Captain Campbell of Barbieston, who often sampled the waters, and he is known to have made his servants drink the waters also. According to William Fullarton of Skeldon, who first became aware of the spring in 1798, the spring was 'a chalybeate, but not strong; also, I believe, a gentle cathartic.' The spring never froze during the winter months.

A man-made chalybeate well in Dalry parish was also used in the late eighteenth century for curing disease. This well was created by a bore hole sunk in the search for new coal seams. The hole was sunk to a depth of nine fathoms, or 54 feet, and from it a strong flow of sulphurous water was obtained. This was used with success in curing 'scorbutic, eruptive and ulcerous disorders, and in stomachic complaints.'

When the Glasgow and South Western Railway was built through the village of Kilwinning an ancient well was destroyed. Known to the locals as the 'Pheesic Well', this spring issued water which was chalybeate in taste. According to the writer of the original *Statistical Account* in 1794, the water was of a considerable benefit to those who laboured under nervous complaints. When the railway was opened through Kilwinning in 1840 the well was covered up, though not before the large circular stone, which had an opening in from where the villagers drank, was rescued and placed in the Manse garden.

Also in Kilwinning is Kyle's Well, which at one time was within the precincts of Kilwinning Abbey, and which may have been blessed by St Winning. In some accounts it is known as St Winning's Well. An ancient tradition claims that this well ran with blood in 1184, as well as at other times just prior to war. The story is ancient, being referred to by R. Hoveden and Benedictus Abbas, and it is claimed that the turning of the water to blood may also have its roots in a Celtic myth. Lord Hailes made reference to the tale of blood from the fountain in his *Annals of Scotland*, which resulted in accusations of incredulity by numerous critics. He stood by his research, however, and in a later impression stated that 'the author must still remain under that imputation, for he cannot submit to acknowledge that he does not believe that a fountain, near Kilwinning, ran blood for eight days and eight nights, without intermission.' However, in 1826 workmen were levelling off the green to the west side of the abbey when they came upon an ancient lead pipe, about one inch in diameter, which ran from the abbey walls to the well. The pipe was noted as having a steep descent, and therefore would not have been used to draw water from the well to the abbey. It was speculated that the pipe was used by abbots to pour animal blood, or a blood-like liquid, in secret from the abbey to the fountain, thereby perpetuating the traditional miracle, and consequently enhancing the fame of the abbey. The well was latterly augmented by a pump, but today is disused and hidden under the floor of a yard. Kyle's Well was originally located just outwith the south western extremity of the glebe, but it was destroyed when the Ardrossan railway line was laid.

A number of wells dedicated to particular saints can still be discovered across the county. St Helen's Well is located at Low Milton farm, near to Minishant, north of Maybole. The well is covered now, but it was originally renowned for its supposed healing powers. At one time hundreds of people gathered there on the first Sunday of May to dip in the waters, believing that they offered a cure for many ills. To those bathing there, it was thought that it was only on the first Sunday in May that the waters had any curative powers. The origins of this belief must have originated in pre-Christian times, but the well was obviously adopted by the monks and named in honour of St Helen. Reference to the well is made in Abercrummie's description of Carrick, written in 1696: 'Another spring … is called St Helen's Well, or by a curt pronuntiation, St Emus for St Antonie's Well. It is about a myle and ane halfe from Mayboll on the road to Aire a little north of Balachmont. It is famous for the cure of unthriving children, to which at the change of the quarter especially at May-day there is a great resort of people from all quarters, and at a good distance.'

St Bride's Well is to be found near to the Craigs of Kyle, south of Coylton. The Bow Burn, a tributary of the Water of Coyle, has its source at the well, which is located 689 feet above sea-level. Little history is known concerning this well, though it is claimed that there was at one time a St Bride's Chapel located in the vicinity, surely a rather high and windswept location for such a place of worship. A few grass-grown rubble walls are located adjacent, however, on the opposite side of the infant stream. The well has been described as a round, stone-lined basin which has been filled with stones, perhaps to prevent cattle, which are the main users of the well today, from falling in and injuring themselves. The water has apparently no curative powers, or at least none is remembered today. The well has been piped into two steel tanks, for use by the nearby farm, as well as a trough for cattle.

At Cloquhairnan farm, which is located just over a mile to the north of St Bride's Well, was an old well known as the Chapel Well, although early accounts name it the Carnell Well. This could be found next to a cottage known as Carnell, which formed part of the hamlet of Barbieston. According to some old accounts there was formerly a chapel here, and it has been claimed that the great Reformer, John Knox, preached here. This connection with Barbieston is perhaps an error, for it probably only comes about from the fact that it was noted that Knox preached at Carnell in Ayrshire, which is more likely to refer to Carnell Castle, in the

MUNGO'S WELL WATER.

Mr JAMES BEGBIE,

BURNS' ARMS INN, ALLOWAY,

RESPECTFULLY intimates, that, at the suggestion of a number of the Inhabitants of Ayr, and with the view of supplying a desideratum which has been long felt, he has now commenced conveying WATER from the above excellent Spring. The Cart will be daily found at the following stations;—

Foot of Barns Street,........	¼ past 7 o'clock	A.M,
Head of Charlotte Street,...	half-past 7 do.	do.
Cathcart Street,.............	8 o'clock	do.
New Bridge,........	quarter past 8	do.
Fish Cross......................	half past 8	do.
Opposite Crown Inn,.....	9 o'clock	do.
End of Mill Vennel,...........	quarter past 9	do.
At the Sheddings,.............	half-past 9	do.

Stopping fifteen minutes at each of the Stations, with the exception of the Fish Cross, where it will remain for half an hour.

Three Imperial Gallons—One Penny.

If Mr B. meets with the encouragement he has been led to expect, the cart may be sent in twice a-day in place of once as at present.

30th July 1839.

3.4 Water from Mungo's Well at Alloway was taken into Ayr and sold, as this handbill shows. *(Author's Collection)*

parish of Craigie. Also in Coylton parish, near to Raithhill, just over one mile west of Barbieston, was another Chapel Well, adjoining which were foundations of a building, supposed to have been a place of worship.

We have already mentioned St Mungo's Well in the Holy Cave near to Portencross in the chapter on caves. The deep well was at one time a popular place of pilgrimage, for its waters were believed to have curative powers.

Another St Mungo's Well is located near to Alloway, on the banks of the River Doon. Mungo was the patron saint of Kirk Alloway, and no doubt the well was the holy well associated with the church. The well gains a greater prominence today by its mention in Robert Burns' *Tam o' Shanter*, in which Tam, fleeing the witches, passed by 'the well, where Mungo's mither hang'd hersel.' There is no tradition of anyone hanging themselves there, and this was probably an elaboration by Burns. At one time fresh water drawn from the well was taken to Ayr High Street and sold.

No longer visible on the ground was St Katherine's Well, which was located by the side of the River Ayr, near to the present Auld Kirk of St John. The well was originally used by the friars of the Dominican Church that formerly stood here, but which appears to have been demolished around 1560, at the time of the Reformation. The well survived for many years afterwards, however, its waters being noted in the burgh for its curative powers. The well was dedicated to St Katherine of Siena, as was the friary, and it appears to have been a place of resort for 'seik maidens'.

Another well, dedicated to St Inan, can be found in Irvine. This is located on the north side of the River Irvine, built into the old glebe wall. The well pre-dates the glebe, and it is circular in shape, over which a stone-built canopy has been constructed. Within the wall is a stone on which is inscribed 'St Inan's Well 839'. Today the well-head has been closed off, so that no access can be made. However, the water still rises from the well, and seeps down to the river. This well was important in the history of Irvine, and is sometimes referred to as St Mary's Well, or the Chapel Well.

By the side of the Burn Anne, or Burnawn, as it is also known and pronounced in the Galston area, can be found the Holy Well. This well

3.5 Sit Inan's Well in Irvine is said to date from AD 839. *(Dane Love)*

is reputed to be named after St Anne, hence the name of the watercourse. It is thought that Anne was the mother of the Virgin Mary. The well is of some antiquity, but it was altered in the Victorian period, when the Duke of Portland utilised it as a source of fresh water for Cessnock Castle, which lies about three quarters of a mile to the west. Thus, visitors today are left with a view of a concrete tank.

St Mary's Well was located near to Hallyards, on the hill road from Dundonald to Loans. The well was associated with St Mary's Chapel, which originally stood at Hallyards, and of which only the littlest of masonry was still to be seen in 1875. The well still ran crystal clear, however, and was a popular spot for slaking one's thirst at one time. Today the site of the old Hallyards farm and St Mary's Chapel has been destroyed by the whinstone quarry, but the spot where the well was survives.

Other wells across Ayrshire associated with saints included Birnie's Well, which was located in Kilbirnie and which was originally dedicated to St Birin. In Beith there was a well dedicated to St Bride, or Brigid. In the north of the county was a well dedicated to St Fillan; this was located to the north of Largs, near the site of an old chapel.

By the side of the Stra Burn, at Auchmannoch, north of Sorn, can be found the Lady's Well. This was a natural spring by the side of the stream, but one that was celebrated in history. Adjacent to the well, which has been built around with stone and is located below a sycamore tree, is a solid sandstone cross, on which is inscribed 'The Lady's Well'

3.6 The Lady's Well at Auchmannoch, in the parish of Sorn, was at one time a 'clootie well' where wishes were made. *(Dane Love)*

in a worn Old English script. Amongst a number of carved inscriptions can just be made out the words 'About AD 1250', which refers to when the well was discovered. This early date associates the well with monks, who probably dedicated the well to the Virgin Mary. Auchmannoch is reckoned to derive from 'Achadh Mannoch', or the field of the monks.

A second tradition associated with the well is that Mary Queen of Scots passed by this way on one of her journeys, perhaps on the day she had lost the field of Langside, for Auchmannoch lies between two known places where she spent the night. At this well she is said to have halted to allow her horses to drink. A few old postcard photographs of the well survive, and on these it is referred to as the 'Wishing Well', indicating that at one time people would make their way to the well, throw in a coin and make a wish. The well also appears to have been a 'clootie well', pilgrims making their way to the well and tying pieces of cloth to adjacent trees and making a wish. This practise seems to have died out around the time of the Second World War. Unfortunately, the well is now virtually dry, for when the roadway to Crofthead farm was being rebuilt, the water supply for the well was disturbed.

The Lady's Well at Kilmaurs is located on the edge of woodland by the side of a small tributary of the Carmel Water. It is claimed that the well was used by nuns to draw water for the original settlement of Kilmaurs, which formerly stood about thirty yards to the west of the well. Today the well comprises a stone-built well-head, opening to one side with a space where a door once was. At one time a small wooden bridge across the Carmel Water allowed visitors to reach the well.

Other wells dedicated to 'Our Lady' formerly existed at Auchinleck. Its location is now unknown, and any tradition associated with it forgotten.

On the slopes of Cairn Table, one of the highest hills on the eastern boundary of Ayrshire, south-east of Muirkirk, can be found a natural spring which has gained the name, Cairn Table Caldron. This is located 1840 feet above sea level, two hundred yards south-west of the summit cairn. The spring flows into a large basin, which an early account of Muirkirk parish, written in 1761, reckons was cut out of the rock. This basin, or trough as the writer describes it, measures twelve feet in length, six feet in width, and was reckoned to be eight feet deep. The basin is always filled with cool spring water, and has gained its place in the local folklore. Some accounts state that the Picts used the basin for soaking stalks of heather, from which they made a delicious drink, often referred to as heather ale. The tradition of heather ale is a popular one in south western Scotland, and it is claimed that the last person to know the recipe for the drink jumped to his death from a Galloway cliff, rather than give it up. There have been hundreds of attempts to recreate this drink over the years, but no-one knows what the original tasted like.

On Fenwick Moor, just over seven miles from Kilmarnock, is the former farm of Kingswell. This name commemorates a story that links the place with either King James V or VI, depending on which writer relates the tale. According to tradition, and there are a number of different versions, the king was invited to a wedding in Ayrshire, and was journeying across the moor from Glasgow when he stopped at a well here for a drink, and from this the place received its name. In later years the King's Well Inn was erected on the spot, catering for other travellers. An additional part of the tale recounts how shortly after leaving the well his horse made its way through a particularly boggy section of the moor, sinking up to its stomach. The horse well and truly stuck in the soft peat, the king had to scramble off and make his way to drier ground. From that day onward this spot was known as the King's Stable, an ironic reference to the sunken horse.

The wedding attended by James V appears to have been either at Loudoun Castle or Sorn Castle, depending on which account is read. At that time Sorn was owned by Sir William Hamilton, the king's treasurer, and it may have been his daughter and heiress who was being married to Lord Seton. King James is supposed to have remarked that 'should he wish to play a trick on the Devil, then he would send him to a bridal at Sorn in the middle of winter!'

Yet another version of the tale behind the naming of the King's Stable is noted in the *Statistical Account* of the parish of Fenwick. There it is claimed that the king, 'one of the James's', was making his way west to settle some disputes at an old castle known as Pokelly, which stood north-west of Fenwick near to the present Pokelly Hall. At the time of the account there were only vestiges of the old tower still visible. En route he halted at Kingswell to rest, whereupon his horse sank into the quagmire. It is said that at Pokelly Castle the king was to hang eighteen miscreants. The place of execution was long pointed out as an ancient hawthorn tree that grew in a field nearby.

Another old story associated with the king's arrival at Pokelly Castle was long told in the neighbourhood. Apparently the king was weary from crossing the Fenwick Moor so he called at a cottar's house to ask for some food. The man of the house was absent, but the gude-wife gave the king some bread and milk to eat, probably the best fare that she was able to provide. As they talked, the gude-wife discovered that the king was going to execute her husband, who was one of the prisoners in the vault at Pokelly Castle. In desperation she pleaded with the king that it would be hard for him to hang a man, 'after he had eaten his breakfast and rested in his arm-chair.' At Pokelly, the king searched out the woman's husband, and let him go with a warning that he was to be a better man in the future.

Within the wooded policies of Chapeltoun House, which sits by the side of the Annick Water, two miles south west of Stewarton, is the Monks' Well. The name Chapeltoun indicates that an ancient chapel at

3.7 The Monk's Well at Chapeltoun House, Stewarton, is associated with an ancient place of worship. *(Dane Love)*

one time existed here, and on the opposite side of the minor road that passes the gatehouse of the mansion can be seen the Chapel Hill, perhaps the spot occupied by the place of worship. Old maps indicate that human bones were found there. The well was probably restored heavily during the Victorian or Edwardian period, for it now has a massive vertical stone slab over it, on which is carved a Christian cross. Through the stone a hole has been cut, which allowed the water to flow from the spring into a cast iron bowl beneath it. Chapeltoun House was erected in 1908-10 by Hugh Neilson, owner of Summerlee Iron Company, and it is possible that he had the current well-head erected as part of the renovations of the immediate policies of the house. Certainly, in 1911 Robert Weir Schultz was consulted in proposals to create a terraced garden. Some others claim that the stone may have been taken from the older Chapeltoun House that was demolished to allow the present house to be erected, and that it was a relic of the original chapel, but this last claim is unlikely.

Another well known as the Monk's Well, or Maak's Well, is located by the side of the Carmel Water, north of the bowling green, in Kilmaurs. Historically, the name was Maak's Well, but by 1831 the Board of Health had changed it to Mack's Well. Locally, the name is often pronounced 'Mank's Well'. Villagers formerly accessed the well by crossing the Carmel by stepping stones, but in 1824 a footbridge was built. At one time the local laird took it upon himself to prevent the locals from drawing water from it. However, soon after he had barred the villagers from using the well, it mysteriously ran dry. The laird was taken aback by this, and consulted one of the local priests. He was advised to, 'Go and restore the well to the people, let them come with their pitchers, and the waters will flow as of yore.' When he announced to the locals that they would be allowed to visit the well once more, the sparkling waters started to flow again.

Yet another Monk's Well could be found within the policies of Glendoune House, which lies to the south-east of Girvan. Glendoune occupies the site of a religious establishment known as Piedmont, and the ancient well used by the monks was long pointed out. Unfortunately, when the railway line was built behind the well, on the slopes of Dow Hill, the source of the water was partially blocked, leaving the well to flow in a much reduced state.

The Chapel Well that lies by the side of the main road north of Dunlop (the A735) is all that remains of an important early ecclesiastical centre. Some think that this was where the pre-reformation centre of the parish was located, whereas others think that it was a secondary chapel to that found in the village. In any case, it is known that there was a chapel dedicated to the Virgin Mary here, possibly erected to replace older buildings used for Christian worship after the pagans who held their services at Thougritstane were converted. It is claimed that the chapel was erected by monks sometime

3.8 The Struil Well is located on a hillside above the ancient kirk ruins of Kirkdamdie, southwest of Barr. *(Dane Love)*

in the twelfth century as an outpost of Kilwinning Abbey. The chapel at one time had an endowment that supported a chaplain, but following the reformation it was abandoned, and gradually fell into ruins. The last ruins were removed a few years prior to 1836.

The Chapel Well, or St Mary's Well as it has also been known, survived, and was still used as a source of water for centuries. Indeed, baptisms in Dunlop church were often performed with water drawn from this well. Some local houses still pump their water from the well, which has been covered over with a concrete cap, complete with manhole, and is not readily visible on the ground. Nearby, across the little Black Burn, were a number of stepping stones, known as 'The Lady's Steps', but these have gone.

On the hillside above the ruins of an ancient chapel, known as Kirk Dandie, or Kirkdominae, can be found a natural spring that is known either as the Struil or Stroll Well. At one time this spring was channelled into a small stone-built house, which contained the holy well of the chapel, and was a place of pilgrimage for the worshippers. In the late nineteenth century the approach to the well was still protected by a stone-built archway, but this was destroyed when a tree collapsed onto it. It was dedicated, like the adjacent kirk, to St Dominae.

At Glendrissaig, near Girvan, is My Fairies' Well. It is located in the glen to the south of the reservoir. The well comprises a small rock cavity which has a pool of water in it, replenished by drips from an overhanging rock. The rock over the well has the words 'My Fairies' Well' painted on it. At one time this well was a common resort for young lovers to walk to from the town. At the well the waters would be drunk and a wish made. J. Kevan MacDowall, writing in *The Carrick Gallovidian*, recalls that, 'In the author's younger days, it was a favourite walk of "a boy and his girl friend" to "My Fairies' Well" of Glendrissaig. There, not only were the crystal-clear and icy cold waters of the "well" tasted and enjoyed but the tasting was accompanied by a silent "wish". During the season, wild strawberries were gathered from several "beds" in the vicinity of the well. These were consumed with relish. Altogether, such a visit to "My Fairies' Well' was a most pleasant experience.'

The Covenanters have been associated with a few wells during the time of the religious struggles of the second half of the seventeenth century. Some of these wells have a tradition that Covenanting ministers performed baptisms at them, often attracting hundreds of infants and young children at the same service. On occasion, Covenanter ministers would let it be known that they intended holding a baptism service at a remote location, and many supporters of the Covenant would make their way across country in order to have their children baptised. Often the children could be quite old, for the Covenanters were unwilling to have them baptised in the Episcopal church. One of the sites that may have been used as a place of baptism by the Covenanters is Peden's Well, which is remotely located by the side of the Water of Tig in south Carrick. The well is located at the foot of the Meikle Glen, in a wooded holm by the side of the Tig.

The name indicates that Rev Alexander Peden, one of the more famous Covenanting ministers, has been associated with the well, and he may have baptised children in its cool waters. Peden is certainly known to have been in the vicinity, for he often stayed with his friend, Hugh Ferguson, at Knockdhu farm, which is located three quarters of a mile to the north. The farm is now little more than a few ruins. On at least one occasion he preached at a spot since known as Peden's Mount, located further up the Water of Tig glen, near to Glenour, or Glenover farm. This is a natural stone projection, from where the 'Prophet' is supposed to have preached. Rev Alexander Peden was captured by the soldiers under Major Cockburn from the Dumfries garrison at Knockdhu in 1673 and was taken from there to Edinburgh, where he was sentenced to imprisonment on the Bass Rock. Hugh Ferguson was subsequently fined 1,000 merks for hiding Peden, and Major Cockburn was awarded £50 for capturing him.

Other wells in the county that have some tradition associated with them, perhaps only their name are listed here. They include St Patrick's Well, which is located on the shore at Croy Bay, north of Culzean Castle. The well is in fact a spring, with a plentiful supply of water. The well was piped in 1932, according to a date stone that formerly existed at it. When the new roadway to the car park at Croy Bay was constructed the well was destroyed, but the water can still be seen seeping onto the sands. The Chapel Well is now located in the midst of the Kyle Forest, south west of Patna. Not too far away, in Glen Muck, south-east of Dalmellington, is the Carrier's Well, no doubt a place where thirsty carriers could refresh themselves and their horses. Maria's Well lies on the Byrebank burn, in the Loudoun castle policies, which runs down near Loudoun Academy to join the Irvine. The well gets its name from being dedicated to St Mary, 'Our Lady'.

King William's Well is to be found in the policies of Rowallan Castle, north of Kilmarnock. Bride's Well, located below a rock cliff on the White Craig of Carrick Hill, is 667 feet above sea level, near to Beoch farm in the parish of Maybole. Whether or not it was named after a bride, or St Bride is no longer known. The Fairy's Well is on the beach at Croy Shore, north of Culzean; another of the same name was to be found at Monkton, between Prestwick and Troon. There is a Lady Well at Culzean, near to Thomaston Castle, and a second at South Threave, in Kirkoswald parish, a couple of miles south-east of Turnberry. The Green Well is located on the moors to the east of Craigdow Hill, south of Maybole. The Dornell Well is in West Kilbride parish, and the Kittyfrist Well is located by the side of the old road south of Girvan that was replaced when the route through Kennedy's Pass was created.

CHAPTER FOUR

TREES and BUSHES

There are certain types of trees that are traditionally connected with superstitions of various sorts. Noted among these is the rowan, which was often planted by the side of a house doorway to ward off evil spirits. Many Ayrshire farmhouses still have rowan trees growing in their immediate vicinity, relics of the times when superstitions were more readily adhered to than they are today. Although many old farmers no longer believe in witches and evil spirits affecting their farm, the rowan is still seen as a tree of luck and many people have an affinity for them.

Small branches taken from the rowan were also used as good luck charms, and such sticks often had a piece of red thread tied around them to add to their effect. An old rhyme recounts this:

Rowan tree and red thread
Keep the devils frae their speed.

Another tree that has many traditional connections was the yew. Noted for its longevity, the yew was associated with immortality – being evergreen – and often was found growing in kirkyards, though perhaps had pagan associations beforehand. At Hunterston an ancient yew tree grows, one that is claimed to be the second oldest yew in Scotland, second only to the oldest in Europe, the yew that grows in the graveyard at Fortingall in Perthshire. The Hunterston yew is said to date from around the year 1110, when the Hunter family were granted their lands. The Hunters were hereditary keepers of the royal forests of Arran and Little Cumbrae, and tradition claims that branches were cut from the yew tree for use in making bows for hunting. The Hunters were confirmed in their lands by a charter of King Robert II dated 2 May 1374, in which it stipulates that they must pay the sovereign one silver penny should he arrive at Hunterston on the Feast of Pentecost to collect it. This rent has not been demanded for many years, but the Hunters still keep a number of silver pennies, minted in the reigns of Robert II and George V, just in case. This type of rent is known as 'blench' payments.

An ancient yew tree grows in the grounds of Loudoun Castle, now a massive ruin to the north of Galston. It was long a seat of the Campbells, Earls of Loudoun. The tree, which grows immediately to the south of the castle, is reckoned to be around 1200 years old, having been measured in 1968 and its age calculated. As such, it is therefore older than the Hunterston yew by many centuries!

Hugh Campbell, 3rd Earl of Loudoun (1667-1731), was a privy councillor to Queen Anne and also to King George I, and Joint Secretary of State for Scotland from 1705. He was selected as one of the Scottish Commissioners who took part in the negotiations which led to the drawing up of the Treaty of Union, which resulted in the union of the Scottish and English parliaments in 1707. Tradition claims that much of the negotiating took place underneath the spreading branches of the ancient Loudoun yew tree, and that some early drafts of the Act of Union were drawn up there. For many years a quill used by the earl to sign the parchment was preserved in the castle.

Loudoun's ancient yew has many tales to tell, some of them unauthenticated, however. It is said that during the time of the Covenanters it was used as a form of Post Office Box – various Covenanters leaving letters within a hollow in the trunk, to be picked up by others during the times when to admit to being a Covenanter was basically to sentence yourself to death. These notes or letters would probably keep the locals up to date with where the next major outdoor services, or conventicles, were to be held, or else to let the families of those Covenanters who had fled to the hills for their safety know that they were well and where they could be found.

It is known that James Campbell, 2nd Earl of Loudoun (d. 1684), used the Loudon yew to contact his family whilst he was in exile at Leyden in Holland. Loudoun had left Scotland in 1654 when he was not included in Cromwell's Act of Indemnity. He was to remain there for thirty years, dying in abroad. During his time in Holland, Loudoun sent a number of letters to his wife, who was able to remain at Loudoun

Castle. The letters were sealed up and the address on them was as follows:

> The Guidwife,
> The Auldtoun,
> The Auld Yew Tree of Loudoun,
> Scotland.

Guidwife is an old Scots term for the mistress or lady of a house, sometimes a landlady, and the term was quite antiquated even then. The Auldtoun was a farm on Loudoun estate, and the farmer's wife at that time was one Mrs Shields, who was able to pass on the letters to their rightful recipient.

The antiquity of the Loudoun Yew, as well as its associations with the history of the Union, prompted one American institution to make an offer of £70,000 to Lady Jean Campbell Hastings, the owner of the estate at the time. They wished to purchase the tree, cut it down and convert it into wooden planks which would be transported abroad and made into smaller novelty souvenirs. Lady Jean refused, despite the estate desperately needing a boost to its funds, claiming that she would never be able to rest easily, thinking that the ghosts of her ancestors

4.1 The churchyard at Old Dailly had ash trees which were associated with a legend. *(Dane Love)*

would haunt her thereafter! Accordingly, the tree survives, still growing healthily in the castle grounds.

There are a few other trees in Ayrshire that have either traditions or legends associated with them. At Old Dailly, in the vale of Girvan Water, are two ash trees. The famous Covenanter, Rev Alexander Peden, is supposed to have prophesised that should the branches of the two trees ever meet, than a great disaster would befall the district. A poem by the local poet, Hew Ainslie (1792-1878), recounted the prophecy:

> When the aishen trees in the kirkyard kiss,
> Happy are the just that that day miss,
> For the French then will come afore it's wist,
> On a morning when the lan's in mist.

The local landowner prevented any great difficulty from attacking Frenchmen under Napoleon by having the trees cut down. However, they subsequently grew again, but have never touched.

In Cumnock's old cemetery, located on Barrhill Road, there grew two hawthorn trees within the railed off enclosure wherein lies Rev Alexander Peden, as well as three other martyrs for the Covenant. The original trees were associated with a legend that was noted in the district. Again, should the branches of these two bushes intertwine, then a great disaster would befall the district. For centuries the two trees had their branches trimmed back considerably. The trees became too old and dangerous and had to be cut down in 1981, but not before cuttings from the trees were propagated. These saplings were able to be planted on the site at a later date, and today have grown into thriving trees.

In the gardens of Glendoune House, which lies outside Girvan, is an ancient tree that local lore claims was planted by Mary Queen of Scots when she passed this way in 1561. The queen is known to have spent two nights at Ardmillan Castle, which stood a few miles to the south, and supposedly planted the tree whilst visiting the local laird. The tree, which has been severely pollarded over the years, still grows, its massive gnarled trunk breaking into a number of huge branches almost immediately it breaks through the ground.

Some of the ancient trees that had legends associated with them have unfortunately either died or been removed, or else have been cut down, so that today no sign of them remains. In many cases the original tree was a victim of old age or severe weather, but the stories associated with them outlasted their existence. Some have even been marked on more detailed Ordnance Survey maps for posterity.

Mention has already been made of Rev Alexander Peden. He was ousted from his church at New Luce in 1663 and spent the next 23 years in hiding, in fear of his life. Although captured on more than one occasion, he actually managed to conceal himself most of his life and died of natural causes near to his brother's farm on Auchinleck estate. One of Peden's hiding places was an old holly tree that grew above the

4.2 Peden's Thorns grow next to his burial place at Cumnock in Ayrshire. *(Author's Collection)*

river Ayr, in the Roughhaugh Wood near to Glenlogan House, near Sorn. Old maps indicate that the tree was located at a different spot in The Glen, but more recent maps located the tree in the wood, where an old holly still flourishes. It is no longer possible to determine which tree was Peden's.

There were many significant trees in the county that were used by the local barons for hanging malefactors and others. Known as 'dule' or 'dool' trees, or various other spellings of a similar-sounding word, virtually every baron had one, and these were often located near to their castle. The name dool derives from the old Scots word for 'sorrow', no doubt a reference to the suffering that the malefactors and their families experienced. Few original dule trees survive, but a number of the sites are known, and in many cases tales associated with them are still related.

Dule trees originated from AD 1057, for in that year Malcolm Canmore, with his parliament assembled at Forfar, enacted that every baron should erect upon his land a gibbet, for the execution of male prisoners. He also decreed that a pit full of water should be available for drowning females.

The dule tree at Cassillis Castle, east of Maybole, was blown over by a severe gale in the winter of 1939-40, leaving only a stump in the ground to mark what had been a very important historical tree. This stump is still visible on the lawns, and a younger tree that has sprouted from it is thought to be of the same provenance as the original dule tree. This was a sycamore tree, known in Scots as the Plane tree. When the original dule tree was blown down the rings on the trunk were counted and it was found to be in excess of 200 years old.

4.3 Cassillis Castle still has the remains of its dule tree growing nearby. *(Author's Collection)*

The dule tree of Cassillis is probably one of the more famous trees in the county, being referred to in an ancient ballad that was very common at one time.

The gipsies cam' to Cassillis yett,
And oh! but they sang sweetly;
They sang sae sweet and sae complete,
That doun cam' our fair lady.

And she cam tripping down the stair,
And all her maids before her;
As sune as they saw her weel-faur'd face,
They cuist the glamourye o'er her.

'Oh, come with me,' says Johnnie Faa.
'Oh, come with me, my dearie;
For I vow and I swear by the hilt of my sword
That your lord shall ne'er come near ye!'

*

And when our lord cam' hame at e'en,
And speired for his fair lady,
The tane she cried, and the tither replied,
'She's away wi' the gypsie laddie.'

'Gae saddle to me the black, black steed,
Gae saddle and mak' him ready;
Before that I either eat or sleep
I'll gae seek my fair lady.'

And we were fifteen weel-made men,
Although we were na bonnie;
And we were a' put down for ane,
A fair young wanton lady.

There are numerous versions of the ballad, and some accounts claim that the incident took place elsewhere in Scotland, but the popular version is as follows.

Johnnie Faa was one of the most important gipsies in Scotland, one of the famous Faa family who were the gipsy kings. He had been in the vicinity of Cassillis Castle when he spotted Lady Jean, the Countess of Cassillis, wife of John Kennedy, 6th Earl of Cassillis. Such was her beauty that he fell in love with her. However, she was already married and unlikely to leave the comforts of her castle to join the travelling people. Johnnie Faa was not to be beaten, however, for he sang from the terrace below the castle up to the window. Lady Jean heard the melodic singing and was attracted to the window. On opening this up to hear the singing better, she noticed that it was Johnnie Faa that was singing.

At length Lady Jean decided to leave her husband and elope with Johnnie Faa. The gipsies regarded her as a great prize, and made much noise by singing and dancing as they left with her. However, the 6th Earl was attracted by the noise and soon discovered that his wife had gone. Accordingly he gathered together a party of men from the estate and they set off in pursuit. It was not too long before they caught up with the gipsy band, and a struggle ensued, in which Johnnie Faa was captured. Lady Jean was also captured and brought back to the ground with a bump, her fanciful notions knocked from her mind.

The Kennedy men dragged Johnnie Faa back to Cassillis Castle where his hands were tied behind his back. A blindfold was placed over his eyes and a noose placed round his neck. The rope was thrown over a branch of the dule tree and the Kennedy men hauled at the loose end of the rope, hanging Johnnie Faa. Lady Jean was kept locked up in a bedroom within the castle, one that overlooked the dule tree, and forced to watch as her lover was hanged. The room in Cassillis Castle that overlooks the tree has been known as the Dule Tree Bedroom ever since.

Lady Cassillis was then taken by her husband to Maybole Castle, in the centre of town, where she was kept locked up for years thereafter. The room in which she was supposed to have been held prisoner is located on the fourth floor, and externally is adorned by a rather well-carved oriel window. Lady Jean is said to have sat by this window-side and gazed over the lands of Carrick, thinking of her hanged gypsy laddie.

It is said that the Earl of Cassillis had the likeness of the gipsies' faces carved in stone and incorporated in the wall of Maybole Castle. Nine effigies are depicted, the face wearing the crown indicating the king of the gipsies. The faces are still there, located around the oriel window.

Another tale associated with the dule tree of Cassillis states that the local members of the Kennedy clan used to gather there when one of their leaders was killed, and thus the tree became a place of grief of a different sort. It is said that for many years the Kennedys were wont to gather there to mark the passing of their chief, and that the last time this took place was in 1513, when David Kennedy, 1st Earl of Cassillis, was slain at the Battle of Flodden, fighting with his king against the English. The Kennedys gathered around the tree and held a wake that lasted for several days.

4.4 Maybole Castle, from where the lady of Cassillis was imprisoned for many years. *(Author's Collection)*

Similarly, in 1527, shortly after Gilbert Kennedy, 2nd Earl of Cassillis, was murdered in the sands of Prestwick by Sir Hugh Campbell of Loudoun, Sheriff of Ayrshire, the Kennedys gathered under the dule tree at Cassillis and together swore an oath that they would avenge the murder. The Kennedys were thereafter to kill a number of the Campbell clan in Ayrshire, including Robert Campbell of Lochfergus. In 1528, 74 members of the Kennedy clan were charged with the murders of the Campbells, but their punishment was limited to fines, so strong were the Kennedys in Carrick that the authorities could not risk any greater penalty.

The dule tree at Blairquhan Castle, near Straiton, still grows, but it has had a rather rough time of it over the centuries. The main trunk of the tree lies at an angle of almost forty-five degrees, and the main branches have been pollarded on more than one occasion, leaving the current tree with two main trunks and numerous smaller branches. This tree is also a sycamore, and it is reckoned that it was first planted sometime in the sixteenth century. The trunk has a girth of around 18 feet 4 inches, but the centre of this has rotted away, leaving it hollow. To prevent the tree from blowing over, the main branches of the tree were cut down in 1997, as the thin rim of the trunk was not likely to support the weight of the crown. The tree still grows, and a new crown of branches flourishes on the old trunk.

The dule tree at Hunterston in West Kilbride parish no longer exists, but a younger tree has been planted on the site. The original tree was an ash, and it grew next to the castle garden, adjacent to the original roadway between West Kilbride and Fairlie. The tree was also known as the 'Hanging Tree', 'Resting Tree' and 'Old Rest Tree'. An old legend associates this tree with one of the sons of the laird of Hunterston. He had spotted a young maiden as she rested beneath the tree and he had fallen for her beauty. He came to her as she lay below the tree, and though he spoke to her she did not reply. At length, in gentle tones, he asked if he may give her a kiss, but as he leaned forward to place a gentle peck on her cheek, she disappeared, never to appear before him again. It turned out that the young woman that he had fallen for was what was known as a 'fairy lass', or fairy taking a female human form.

A plaque adjacent to a later tree relates some interesting details about the original tree:

> The Hunterston Resting Tree stood beside this wall for many years. A seat, where travellers could rest, was placed within the hollow trunk. In 1985 an oak seedling from Goldenberry Wood was planted here by Neil Aylmer Hunter, 29th Laird of Hunterston and Chief of the Clan Hunter.

At Newark Castle, south of Ayr, a large dule tree grew near to the main stair tower. This tree was an ash and it was measured in the mid nineteenth century as having a circumference of around fifteen feet. Five principal branches came from the bole, and it still grew in 1864 when James Paterson describes it as 'altogether beautifully proportioned'. In 1895 John Smith, writing in *Prehistoric Man in Ayrshire*, recorded that the stump of this dule tree was carefully preserved.

The dule tree at Auchendrane was conserved to some extent – it was manufactured into various items of furniture! The tree was an ash of some age, but it was blown over sometime prior to 1864 and the timber was sold to a cabinet-maker in Maybole. This man manufactured a number of chests of drawers from the wood once it had seasoned.

This tree played an important part in the feuds of the Mures of Auchendrane and the Kennedys of Carrick. These feuds were versified by Sir Walter Scott in his *Auchendrane, or the Ayrshire Tragedy*, written in 1830. In the preface Scott tells of how the last of the family fell into pecuniary circumstances and was arrested for his debts:

> This last representative of the family of Auchindraine had the misfortune to be arrested for payment of a small debt; and, unable to discharge it, was preparing to accompany the messenger (bailiff) to the jail of Ayr. The servant of the law had compassion for his prisoner, and offered to accept of this remarkable tree as value adequate to the discharge of the debt. 'What!' said the debtor; 'Sell the Dule-tree of Auchendraine! I will sooner die in the worst dungeon of your prison!'

The old dule tree adjacent to Cessnock Castle, near to Galston, is a sweet chestnut. This tree is still in existence and stands a gnarled example. Kilkerran House, which stands in the vale of Girvan Water, north-east of Dailly, still has an ancient dule tree growing in the policies. In the same valley, near to Bargany House, the dule tree was a European Ash.

There were two holly trees growing at either end of an ancient gravestone located remotely by the side of the Noddsdale Water, in the Brisbane Glen, north-east of Largs. These trees had a tradition going back to the seventeenth century, at a time when the district was ravaged by plague. The plague hit Largs in 1647, first noted in the records of the Presbytery of Irvine for 29 June that year. The minister, Rev William Smith, was killed by the disease, and the presbytery noted on 28 September 'the lamentable and calamitous condition of the paroch of Largs, partly by reason of the hand of God that is lying heavy upon them, and partly by reason of their minister by death, thinks it expedient that Mr Wm. Lindsay be sent to visit them, and to take notice of their desires, and to enquire ane overture of themselves how they may be gotten helpit and supplied; and the said Mr Wm. to make report of his diligence.'

Things seem to have got worse, and on 26 October the presbytery minutes noted the following:

> The laird of Bishopton having remonstrate the calamitous condition of the parish of Largs, and the present necessity that the town of Largs was in, and that if it were not tymouslie removit and helpit, the people wald be forcit to break out athort the countrie. The Presbyterie, after hearing, ordains that these bretheren of the Presbiterie, who, upon the report of their present necessity, had already gathered something for supply of the same, should presentlie apply themselves for their relief, either in money or in victual, as suld be thought most expedient, and that the rest of the bretheren sould use all possible diligence in collecting a contribution to be sent to them to refresh them in their necessity.

The aid gathered from surrounding parishes was considerable – Newmilns sent £700 8s 4d; Irvine sent 200 merks, Kilmaurs sent 102 merks, Stewarton contributed £111, Kilwinning collected £100, and the parish of Pearston sent £40 and 8 merks.

William Smith played an important part in Largs' struggle against the plague. He was inducted to the town in 1644 and was a gifted preacher, being much-liked by the parishioners. He visited many of those who suffered from the plague, and as a result contracted the disease himself. He died in September 1647, aged around 28 years. As he was never married, 'he had no cowes, cattel, nor uther moveable guides, except allenerlie certaine small insycht and plenishing of his chalmers, with his buikis and abuilzements of his body.' Smith's wishes were that he should be buried in the Noddsdale valley, near to Middleton farm, where he had died. Accordingly a flat stone was placed over his grave in a woody hollow. Local tradition claims that on his deathbed, Smith was heard to say that so long as the two holly trees that grew either side of his chosen resting place did not meet, then the plague would never again return to Largs. This prophecy resulted in Smith's burial spot becoming known as 'The Prophet's Grave'.

The old stone bore the inscription:

> Heir layeth M William Smith, minister of Larges, a faithful minister of the gospell, removed by the pestilence 1647. Conditus in tumulo hoc jaceo juvenisque senexque; nempe annis juvenis, sed pietate senex, Divino eloquio, coelestia dogmata vidi abstersi tenebras, mentibus, ore tonans. Altoniloque haesit animo per vera malorum colluvies, verbis improba facto meis. Renewed by James Smith, his nephew, in the year 1710. Renewed 1760.

4.5 The Prophet's Grave near Largs marks the resting place of the local minister who died at the time of the plague. *(Dane Love)*

The inscription is mostly illegible, but the inscription was copied from the tombstone at the restoration of the site in 1956 when a plaque was added by Largs Business Club in conjunction with St Columba's Parish Church.

In Largs there was an old hawthorn tree known as the Reformer's Tree. This was located near to the mound up the Gogo glen on which stood the three pillars used for aligning the telescope from the observatory at Brisbane. The tree got its name from it being used to hang the target at which dart-like objects, known as 'clegs' were thrown. At the time the tree was used, reform of the government was demanded by many residents of towns and burghs, resulting in riots in a number of places. Weavers were among the main supporters of reform, and in Largs they often gathered here to practise their aim. It was the case that weavers and other reformers thought that they could throw their 'clegs' from the upper floor windows of buildings in the towns if and when government soldiers rode past.

A number of ancient trees had a tradition that someone hid within their hollow trunks, or amid their branches. Many of these fabled trees have succumbed due to their age over the centuries, and most of the old stories seem to have died with them

Near to Barr Castle, in Galston, grew an ancient elm tree. It stood just outside the garden of the castle, which in recent years has had a number of private houses built in it, but the old garden wall still survives. At the time of Paterson's *History of Ayrshire*, written in 1852, the tree still appears to have existed and was known locally as 'The Warrior's Tree'. It was dead by that time, however, and only the arid trunk and withered branches remained.

The 'warrior' referred to the tradition that Sir William Wallace at one time hid himself amongst the great branches of the tree. When Paterson noted the tree he describes the main trunk as being hollowed out, and it was sufficiently large to allow several people to hide within it.

Archibald Mackay, who wrote a history of Kilmarnock in 1848, also wrote a book of poems entitled *Recreations of Leisure Hours*, published in 1844. In it he refers to the tree in one of his verses:

The vision had passed, but the warrior's tree,
Though fading 'neath Time's chilling blight,
Still Waves its broad branches alone on the lea,
The haunt of brave Wallace the Wight.

The Battle of Dettingen took place at Dettingen in Bavaria on 27 June 1743, when the British army fought against the French over the Austrian line of succession. The battle was a victory for the British, and it was so important in the minds of the people at the time that it was commemorated across the country. It was also a significant battle in that it was the last time the reigning monarch, in this case George II, was active on the field. At two places, at least, in Ayrshire the landowners even went to the length of laying out their grounds in battle formation, planting trees to represent the armies.

The largest example of this method of commemorating the battle was carried out in Old Cumnock parish, where William Crichton, 4th Earl of Dumfries, planted trees to celebrate his part in the war. Just west of Cumnock, by the side of the present roundabout at the junction of the A76 and A70, is a circular wood known as the Dettingen Wood, or Mount. From it the roundabout was given the name Dettingen Roundabout, something that has caused interest amongst many travellers passing through. The Dettingen Wood occupies a low knoll, and comprises a perfect circle around 215 yards in diameter. The wood was planted to represent the French army prior to commencement of the battle.

4.6 The 2nd Earl of Stair, who planted trees in the formation of the Battle of Dettingen. *(Dane Love)*

To the south west, three quarters of a mile away, is a second round wood, not just as large, measuring 200 yards in diameter, representing a smaller troop. This wood is known as the Stair Mount, after John Dalrymple, 2nd Earl of Stair (1673-

1747), uncle of Lord Dumfries, who led the British army in the battle until the king nominally assumed control. When the woods were originally planted they comprised beech trees, which must have formed a magnificent sight when they had fully grown, but over the years they have been cut down and replaced with softwood trees, much to the wood's detriment.

Lord Stair planted trees to mark the battle himself, though in his case he only planted single specimens in the fields around Stair House. Just one of these trees still survives – a large beech tree near to Stair Parish Church known as 'The General', having been planted to represent Field Marshall Stair. Lord Stair also owned Lochinch Castle near Stranraer at this time, and he planted woods to commemorate the battle there. Thus, on the slopes of Balker Hill, is a second Dettingen Wood.

4.7 The Trysting Thorn between Laigh Coylton and Drongan has associations with Robert Burns. *(Dane Love)*

At Montgarswood, in the parish of Sorn, the victory over the French at the Battle of Waterloo on 18 June 1815 was celebrated by the laird of what was a small estate at that time. He planted a number of trees in battle formation on his lands, but these trees have unfortunately long been obliterated.

At Thirdmailing, in the parish of West Kilbride, at one time grew an ancient and gnarled ash tree known as the Witch's Ash Tree. It was said in 1896 that many of the older residents of the parish could recall tales of the tree in their youth, and that they were frightened when they passed by its hoary branches. Few stories associated with the tree appear to have survived, other than speculation that there may have been a murder committed in its vicinity, or else that some of the victims of the plaque of 1665 were buried at the foot of it. The tree had either been cut or blown down by the end of the twentieth century.

The Trysting Thorn grows by the side of the road near to Millmannoch, between Laigh Coylton and Drongan. Old illustrations show it as being a rather straggly hawthorn tree, not dissimilar to any one of thousands of bushes that abound in Ayrshire. The tree was referred to by Robert Burns in his poem, 'The Soldier's Return'. This makes reference to a soldier who had fought in the battles abroad and was returning home to Scotland. He was probably a soldier with the Royal North British Fusiliers who had depots in Ayr and Dumfries.

The Trysting Thorn eventually succumbed to old age and died. The miller at Millmannoch at the time was James Pearson Wilson (1872-1954), a local antiquarian. Recognising the worth of the tree, he had the dead trunk cut down and chopped into segments. These were sent to the Mauchline box works where they were fabricated into gavels and small plaques. Each one had the verse by Robert Burns added to them, and these were distributed to various Burns Clubs around the world:

At last I reached the bonnie glen,
Where early life I sported,
I passed the mill and trysting thorn,
Where Nancy aft I courted.

The site of the old trysting thorn tree had a new hawthorn tree planted, and a set of iron railings were erected around it to protect the new growth. The tree has re-established itself, and at the time of writing is still growing strongly.

At one time an ancient tree grew within the policies of old Rowallan Castle, north of Kilmarnock. The tree was located at the top of a steep bank by the side of the Carmel Water, known as Janet's Kirn. This was upstream from the old castle. At the close of the seventeenth century Rowallan Castle had an heiress, Dame Jean Mure, who was not only good-looking, but was soon to inherit a large estate and ancient castle. Therefore, she was much suited by would-be husbands, but none of them were to her liking. One man, however, she loved, and he was William Fairlie of Bruntsfield, who owned a small estate near Edinburgh. Little more than a bonnet-laird, Fairlie was not thought of as being good enough by her father, and therefore his request of marriage was turned down.

The path of true love was not to be broken, however, and at length Lady Jean decided that she would elope. One night, when all were asleep in the castle, she climbed from a small window down to the courtyard. This window is still pointed out on the building. Fairlie met his bride, and the pair headed off across the Carmel Water. Anticipating that perhaps Lady Jean's father may be awakened and pursue them, he came prepared with a minister in tow. Once the threesome had travelled around 1200 yards from the old tower, they stopped at the large tree. There, under its spreading branches, the minister, a curate, performed the marriage ceremony before anyone could come between the lovers. For centuries the 'Marriage Tree' continued to grow by the Carmel, but it has long-since fallen.

Another legendary tree that no longer exists is the Bickering Bush, which grew near to the side of the River Irvine, just west of Riccarton. The hawthorn bush had historic associations with Sir William Wallace. One day the freedom fighter was fishing in the River Irvine and was able to land a fair catch of salmon and other fish. With a heavy load, he was walking back to the castle of Riccarton, at the time the home of his uncle, Sir Ronald Crawford. A party of English soldiers were passing at the time and spotted Wallace with the fish. They demanded that he should hand them over, but Wallace refused. An argument ensued, and one of the English soldiers dismounted to start a brawl with Wallace. In the fight Wallace was able to use his fishing rod to disarm the knight, and using the enemy's own sword decapitated him. The other English soldiers, despite outnumbering Wallace, decided to flee, rather than risk their own lives in the affray. Wallace, however, would not give in, and pursued for a while, managing to kill another two of the enemy. The spot where the fight had taken place was near to an old thorn bush, known as the 'Bickering Bush' from that time onward.

Wallace then made his way back to Riccarton Castle as quick as he could. Within at the time was only the housekeeper, who immediately feared that the English would attack, looking for Wallace. She ordered the freedom fighter to put on a mutch and a long gown, and sit himself down at a spinning wheel. As expected, the soldiers came to the castle looking for Wallace. The housekeeper told them that the castle was empty, save for herself and her sister. The soldiers looked around, and agreed with her, before leaving.

The Bickering Bush survived for many years, before succumbing due to its age. In 1822, when it had perished, the timber was saved and cut into smaller parts, which were subsequently made into souvenirs. Whether or not any of these survive is unknown, but in 1879 a James Paxton is known to have owned a snuff box that was inscribed with the information that it had been made from the bush.

In front of the fire station at Riccarton is a small memorial containing a stone recording that it occupied the site of Riccarton Castle. At one time, prior to redevelopment in the area, there was a small inn or public house, known as 'The Bickering Bush', recalling the tale. This pub was demolished in the 1980s.

The road from Auchinleck to Ochiltree, now the B7036, is known as the Barony Road, at least the straight section from Auchinleck west towards Auchinleck estate is. The road was originally laid out by Alexander Boswell, Lord Auchinleck (1706-1782) as a new route from his country seat at Auchinleck House to the parish church in Auchinleck. Lord Auchinleck had been instrumental in making considerable improvements to his estate, for he established Auchinleck as a planned village, with new cottages on a regular street layout, he erected a new country house in the classical style to replace the old tower house, and he built many new farmhouses and improved the land around them.

The Barony Road appears to be virtually straight from the gatehouse at Auchinleck House to the vicinity of Auchinleck village, at Highhouse. However, if one looks at a map one can see that the route is not straight at all, but takes the form of three sections of straight road. The westmost, from the gatehouse to where the Barony 'A' frame is located, is 1450 yards in length, the central section, east to the Hapland Plantation is 1000 yards long, and the eastmost to Hill Cottage, is also 1450 yards in length. Lord Auchinleck referred to the road as the 'Via Sacre', or sacred road, being the route he took to the church.

4.8 The trees alongside the Barony Road, Auchinleck, were planted to commemorate the Boswell family. *(Dane Love)*

What makes the Barony Road quite unique was the use of trees grown alongside to form a two and a half mile avenue. The trees, beech and oak, were planted repeatedly in that order along both sides of the road. The initial letters of each tree – B and O – formed the first two letters of the name Boswell. Over the years a number of the trees have become dangerous and have had to be cut down, whereas others have died naturally and fallen. In many places other trees have sprung up, often the self-seeding sycamore, leaving the avenue less refined.

A second story is told of the Barony Road. At the east end of the route, in the village of Auchinleck, were a number of miners' rows, known as the Highhouse Rows. These were built in 1894-6 when Highhouse pit was sunk, the horrals of which still survives to mark the site of the mine in what is now a small industrial area. When the miners' houses were being erected it is said that the Boswells, who still owned Auchinleck, insisted that the front door of the houses should be located on the opposite side of the house from the Barony Road. No doorway was to be located on the road side, which was a considerable inconvenience to the occupiers. It was said that this was the case because the Boswells did not wish the miners nor their families to stand at their front doors and watch as they went to the church. The Highhouse Rows were demolished in 1959, but some of the rear walls remained for a number of years, and the bricked up windows and absence of doors could still be made out. Only one of these rear walls remains at the time of writing.

CHAPTER FIVE

BELTANE and BONFIRES

Prior to the arrival of Christianity to Ayrshire, the county was pagan in its beliefs, and various forms of worship were practised, be it either worshipping the sun or some such natural feature. One of the most common traditional festivals was Beltane, or *Bealltainn*, when fires were burned on the first day of May to celebrate the arrival of the summer. In the old Celtic calendar, Beltane was the second most important festival in the year, the other being *Samhainn*, held on 1 November. In later years the year was divided into four, adding *Imbolc* (on St Bride's Day, 1 February) and *Lughnasad* (on Lammas day, 1 August). Beltane was important as it was at this time the cattle were moved from around the farmhouse, or within the byre, out onto the open grazings.

The use of bonfires to celebrate Beltane was taken a stage further in superstition, for two smaller fires were often lit and the cattle driven between them. This was supposed to protect the cattle from various diseases. In some areas, such as the highlands of Scotland, these fires could be quite distant, located on separate hill-tops. It was also traditional that on Beltane the fires in houses were extinguished, to be rekindled from the purifying flame of the Beltane bonfire. However, the burning of bonfires seems to have been a tradition that could take place at any time throughout the year, from summer to Christmas.

In the *Statistical Account* of the parish of Loudoun, written in 1791, it was noted then that 'the custom still remains amongst the herds and young people to kindle fires in the high grounds, in honour of Beltan. *Beltan*, which in Gaelic signifies *Baal*, or *Bel's-fire*, was antiently the time of this solemnity. It is now kept on St Peter's Day.'

Henry Richmond of East Montgarswood farm, in the parish of Sorn, kept a diary from 1823 until 1824 that has survived, and which was replicated in part in *On an Ayrshire Farm*, by John Strawhorn. Richmond was aware of Beltane and its older significance, for he noted in his journal of 12 May 1823:

> This is what old people call Beiltan Day, a festival among the ancient Caledonians whereon they kindled bonfires in honour of some of their deities. Old people still speak of Beltan that know nothing about its derivation, but make it a rule to drive their cattle to pasture on this day. Our cattle were turned out today, accordingly.

In Dalry parish the traditional burning of bonfires on the last day of July continued well into the nineteenth century. No doubt this ceremony had its roots in the pagan fire festivals, but the saints had converted early parishioners to Christianity and the bonfires were now to be held on what was St Margaret's Day – St Margaret being the saint to whom the old chapel of Dalry was dedicated, as well as the name of the present parish church. The locals called the bonfires that they lit on that day a 'baal fire', which is probably a corruption of Beltane. The festival was also known as 'Tannel', which is thought to derive from the old Scots *tandle*, meaning bonfire. This word probably derives from the Gaelic *teine*, which means 'fire'.

For a few weeks prior to St Margaret's Day, the boys of Dalry parish would wander around, carrying large horns, into which they would ask the parishioners for a contribution with which to buy coal for the 'baal fire'. At one time the boys would have been led by a piper, and as he played the pipes the audience danced a reel around the bonfire. Writing in the *New Statistical Account* in 1836, Thomas Hogg of Toftsmill noted that the presence of a piper had 'fallen into desuetude.' Nevertheless, the boys gathered funds and purchased coal. Bonfires were built and on St Margaret's Day they were lit. It was also a tradition to dance a reel around the fire, but again this part of the tradition died out. Today, the whole ceremony has become extinguished, just like the bonfires themselves!

In Irvine bonfires were frequently lit throughout the sixteenth, seventeenth and early part of the eighteenth century. The burgh accounts note that in 1661 considerable ale, wine and glasses were purchased at a cost of £10 10s 8d for the hospitality adjoining the bonfire. In 1681 ten loads of coal were used for a bonfire, costing £3 3s 4d. The town's historic Marymass festival, held on the first Saturday after the third Monday in August, also had a bonfire in its early days, known locally as the 'tandle'. It was also described as a 'bane-fire', another old Scots term for bonfire.

Hoods Hill at Tarbolton is an ancient motte and bailey, the site of the earliest of castles, where a timber palisade was erected on top of a man-made mound. Long after the timber wall had rotted away, the mound remained, and it became a notable feature in the village. On the summit of the hill bonfires were lit annually, to celebrate the worship of Baal. In later years the fire was Christianised, and the hill became the site of the annual June Fair.

5.1 The ancient motte hill at Tarbolton also used as the site of the local bonfire at the annual Beltane festival. *(Dane Love)*

Rev David Ritchie, despite being minister of the church in Tarbolton, seems to have taken some delight in ascribing his parish to being named after the pagan gods, so that Tarbolton perhaps means Torr, or hill, of Beltane. The festival of the bonfire is described with a keenness unbecoming a Presbyterian minister of period:

> Some superstitious rites, anciently observed in honour of this eastern god, are annually performed on the hill. One evening preceding the Torbolton June fair, a piece of fuel is demanded at each house, and is invariably given even by the poorest inhabitant. The fuel so collected is carried to a particular part of the hill, where there is an altar or circular fire-place of turf, about three feet in height, and is placed upon the altar. A huge bonfire is kindled, and many of the inhabitants, old and young, men and women, assemble on the hill and remain for hours, apparently chiefly occupied with observing a feat performed by the youths, who are to be seen leaping with indefatigable zeal upon the altar or turf wall, inclosing the ashes of former fires, and supporting the present one. It appears from sacred Scripture, that the worship of Baal consisted in part of leaping upon his altar; 'And they leaped upon the alter which was made.' (1 Kings, xviii, 25).

In Prestwick, bonfires seemed to play a significant part in the annual festivities in the town. The town had an annual 'Bonfire Monday', held on the first Monday in July, on the week preceding Ayr's Midsummer Fair. Local herd-laddies went around the burgh gathering donations of halfpennies which paid for their efforts in building the bonfires. Using this money they purchased bread and cheese to keep them going, and any spare pocket money was spent at the stalls of itinerant craftsmen. By the late nineteenth century Bonfire Monday had almost died out, only being marked by the younger members of the community, to whom large bonfires held a special appeal. Bonfires continued to be lit in the early years of the twentieth century, but the festival had died out by the time of the Great War, which brought an end to many traditional events.

A local poet, R. MacKenzie Fisher, wrote of Prestwick's Bonfire Monday in his book, *Poetical Sparks:*

When the bonfire took place in the month o' July,
And the herd laddies gather'd bawbees through the toon,
On our help and attention they aye could rely,
Till the scenes were all ower and the bonfire burnt doon.

Writing in *A Little Scottish World*, Rev Kirkwood Hewat recalled some of the activities that took place in Prestwick on Bonfire Monday:

> Round these bon-fires the people have been wont to meet annually for centuries, though the practice is now very much confined to the juvenile section of the community. They danced and shouted, it was said, for the purpose of keeping away the witches. It is in mid-summer – on St John's eve – that these bon-fires are lighted, and the occasion is something like a local festival. Many affirm that this is a relic of the old Pagan worship. Tarbolton, which is said to mean *the hill of Baal's town*, is generally credited with having relics of the old worship, and in this district – its neighbouring parish – it is very probably there would be relics also; and many have looked upon the Mid-Summer Festival of Fire as a relic of the old Baal worship. The word 'Beltan' occurs in the Burgh Records.

John MacIntosh, writing in 1894, noted that Beltane, near the end of its popularity, was mainly celebrated by cow-herds. They were wont to assemble on the summit of hills near to the village and kindle bonfires. The cow-herds also cooked a meal comprising boiled eggs and milk on the fire and ate them with a special type of cake that was baked for the occasion. It is thought that the cake may have originally formed some form of offering to the deity in the time of paganism.

There survive a number of places across Ayrshire, in particular the northern half of the county, which have the name Tandle Hill. One of these can be found at Threepwood, on the east side of the parish of Beith. The hill stands above Threepwood House, almost 160 feet above sea level. Almost two and a half miles to the south, to the east of Barrmill village, is Tandlehill farm. Although located on the brow of an eminence, this hill is nowhere as high or as prominent as other tandle hills, indeed, the countryside tends to rise to the east, reaching a summit at High Gree.

The term 'Law Hill' also seems to have had some connection with bonfires. According to Rev Thomas Maxwell, who wrote in the *Statistical Account* of the parish of Stewarton, there are a number of small hills in that parish which bear the name Law Hill. He speculated that this was 'either because that in olden times courts of justice were held upon them, or from the low or flame raised on them, as a signal of the approach of an enemy.'

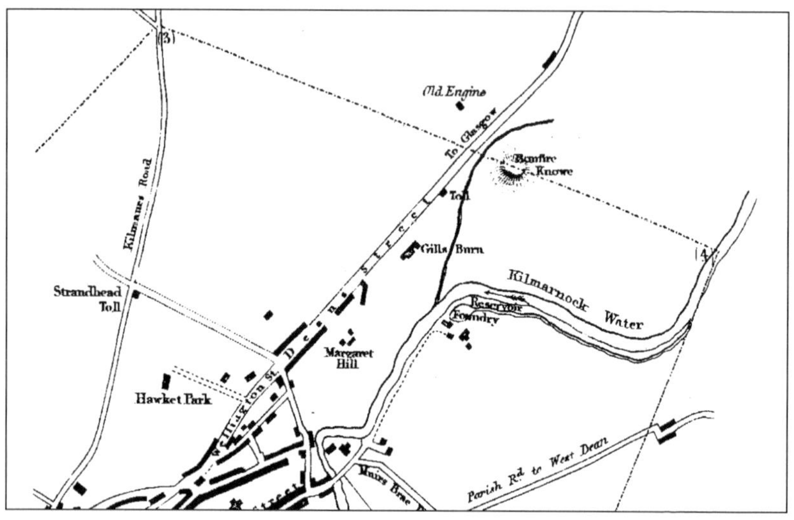

5.2 The Bonfire Knowe at the top end of Kilmarnock was used as a marker point for the burgh boundary. *(Author's Collection)*

A number of towns had their own bonfire site that was used over the centuries, and which, like Tarbolton, probably had a turf or stone ring around them. In Kilmarnock, the old bonfire site was located at the north end of the town, near the junction of Dean Road with Beansburn, and in 1832 the burgh boundary included the site as one of the ten points forming the extremity of the burgh lands. The Bonfire Knowe was later known as Dean Hill. In Prestwick the Bonfire Hills were located to the north of St Quivox Road, on what was Prestwick Moor. With 'Bonfire Monday' a thing of the past, and pressure of development, they were flattened in the early twentieth century to allow the erection of houses in what is now Broompark Avenue.

With their roots in Pagan festivals, Beltane was much disliked by the parish ministers. They despised the fun and frivolity of taking part in the building and burning of bonfires. Trying to prevent Beltane bonfires had been the object of authority ever since the arrival of Christianity. As early as the seventh century, St Kentigern, or St Mungo as he was also known, tried to stop the festival. At a later period, in the late fifteenth century, the Lollards of Kyle tried to prevent them from taking place.

In 1582, King James VI, through the Scottish Parliament, passed an act that was designed to suppress bonfires, and other superstitious customs and locations. The act runs:

> For-sa-meikle, as pairtlie for the want of Doctrine, and raritie of Ministeris, and pairtlie throw the preverse inclination of Man's ingine to superstition, the dregges of Idolatrie zit remaines in divers pairtes of the Realme, be using of Pilgrimages to some Chapelles, Welles, Croces, and sik uther monuments of Idolatrie. As also observing of the Festival dayes of the Sanctes, sumtime named their Patrones, in setting furth of bane-fyers, singing of Carralles, within and about Kirkes, at certaine seasons of the zeir, and observing of sik uther superstitious and Papistical Rites, to the dishonour of God, contempt of his true Religion, and fostering of great errour amang the people. For remeid quhairof, It is statute and ordained be our Soveraine Lord, with advice of his three Estaites of this present Parliament, That nane of his Hienes Lieges presume or take upon hand in time cumming, to haunt, frequent or use the saidis Pilgrimages, or uthers the foir-named superstitious and Papistical Rites, under the paines following, videlicet, Ilk Gentil-man or Woman landed, or Wife of the Gentil-man landed, ane 100. pundes. The unlanded ane hundreth markes, and the Zeamen [Yeomen] fourtie pundis, for the first fault. And for the second fault, the offenders to suffer the paine of death as Idolaters. And for the better execution
> heirof, Commandis, ordainis and gives power to all

> Schireffes, Stewartes, Baillies, Provestes, Aldermen, and Baillies of Burrowes, Lords of Regalities, their Stewartes and Baillies, and utheris, quhome it sall please our Soveraine Lord to grant special Commission, to searche and seeke the persons, passing in Pilgrimage to ony Kirkes, Chapelles, Welles, Croces, or sik uther monuments of Idolatrie.

Celebratory bonfires at Beltane became prohibited by this act of parliament, and rather severe punishments were meted out to those who took part in the festivities. These rules were brought in following the Reformation, for the Protestant clergy regarded them as being relics of paganism – something that should be got rid of. Graded fines, depending on one's rank or income, were exacted, and regular offenders could even be punished by death, guilty of idolatry.

Dousing the Beltane bonfire was something that was extremely difficult for the authorities to enact. The country folk felt that since they had burned fires on the first of May for centuries, then they had every right to continue. Most of these folk were Christian in any case, and they could see no wrong in starting fires, especially as they had no intention of worshipping other gods. They were just having a good time! As a result, bonfire building, especially around May and June, continued for many centuries after the Reformation, and it is only in recent years that the festivals have died out, bonfires only being constructed now to celebrate Guy Fawkes' Night.

A case in Muirkirk from 1664, though it does not mention a bonfire as such, scandalised the local kirk session. It was May, hence the possibility that the incident had connections with Beltane, and the culprits had made their way to the top of Middlefield Law, north of the village. It was then that 'ane grosse scandall' was committed on a Sabbath day after the sermon. Bessie Jamy, Jonat Jamy, Jonat Duncan, Agnes and Bessie Beges, left their homes and made their way to the top of the hill. There they carried on in 'loupenis and discoursing most unbecoming ane sabboth day.' The ladies had been betrayed by two men, but what their punishment was is not recorded in the minute book.

It was not only at Beltane that bonfires were lit on the summits of various hills across the county. It is recorded that in Galston parish bonfires were lit on the day before the annual St Peter's Fair, which was originally held on 29 June. Why this was so is not known, but on the evening before the fair took place, locals piled up wood and bushes on surrounding hill-tops and set them ablaze, the flames leaping into the summer sky. It has been speculated that this bonfire tradition may have been the remnants of the druidical festival that celebrated the summer solstice. St Peter's Fair seems to have become less popular by the end of the eighteenth century, but bonfires were still lit at that period.

There was also a tradition of bonfires being set alight on high hilltops to warn of invasion. In times of war, piles of wood were kept at the ready on elevated tracts of ground. If any enemy should invade, the fires would be lit, sending a light across country, passing on the news quicker than any runner could take it. Ayrshire, like the rest of the country, has a tradition of bonfire hills, many of which are still known.

Loudoun Hill, at the east end of the county, on the boundary with Lanarkshire, is one of the better known bonfire hills. Indeed, the name Loudoun is said to derive from 'the hill of flame'. Similarly, at the south-eastern corner of the county, on the boundary with Dumfriesshire, is the hill known as Corsencon, again a prominent hill-top with extensive panoramas. Should any foreigner have invaded these shores then these hills were where the news arrived into the county.

In the parish of Ardrossan are two prominent hills, Knock Jargon (or Knock Georgan) and Roundhill. In the *Statistical Account* it is claimed that a fire was lit on the top of the burial cairn at a time when the 'Danish fleet were seen advancing towards the shore', a reference to Viking invaders. 'From these two hills,' so the *Account* continues, 'by smoke in the day, and by flame in the night, signals were communicated from hill to hill till the whole inland country was alarmed.'

Bonfires have been lit in various locations across the county to celebrate many events over the centuries, and they still take place on occasion to this day. On 8 August 1878 a bonfire was lit in Irvine's Bank Street to celebrate the opening of the public water supply. The fire was kept blazing for much of the night.

Similarly, significant victories by the British forces were marked by bonfires. The victory at Waterloo in 1815 was marked by many bonfires being lit across the country, often on hilltops. In Prestwick the victory of the British over the Boers at the Relief of Ladysmith in February 1900 was marked by a huge bonfire.

In recent years certain events have resulted in bonfires being built across the county. One of the more significant and better co-ordinated bonfire nights took place to celebrate Queen Elizabeth's Silver Jubilee, which took place in 1977. A chain of bonfires, much as was used in the past to warn of invasion, was set up across the country, and Ayrshire was no exception. Bonfires for this event were built and lit on many summits, including Loudoun Hill at the east end of the Irvine valley, and Corsencon Hill, guarding Ayrshire's boundary with Nithsdale.

CHAPTER SIX

FAIRIES and OTHER MYTHICAL CREATURES

Fairies, or little people, were at one time greatly believed in throughout the area. A peculiarly Ayrshire term for fairies appears to be 'fane', which is no doubt a pluralisation of the old term 'fay', meaning fairy. Jamieson's *Scottish Dictionary*, states that 'fane' is an old Ayrshire word meaning fairies, but the earliest reference to it known to the compiler was written by Joseph Train (born in Sorn parish) who used it in his *Poetical Reveries*, published in 1806. Chambers' *Scots Dictionary* described 'fane' as meaning either elf or fairy.

Fairies also came in an evil guise. They often seem to have shown some ill-will against certain farms, and one of their favourite tricks was to cause the butter churns to fail. No matter how hard or long the churn was tumbled, the milk within failed to turn into butter. This was often cited as evidence that the bad fairies had placed a spell on the farm, and the churn was useless thereafter. There was one way of clearing the spell, however, and that was to wash it in water which was to be found where three lairds' land met. One such spot was to be found in the parish of Old Cumnock, located on the opposite side of the road from the gate-house to Glaisnock House. At that point the lands of Lord Bute marched with the estates of Skerrington and Glaisnock. The actual junction was in a pool in the Meadow Burn, and many churns were washed there to rid them of their curse.

Cleeves Cove is a natural cave located in a limestone gorge of the Dusk Water, south east of Dalry. In thickly wooded Dusk Glen, the cave is situated around forty feet above the level of the stream. There are two entrances to the cavern, the main entrance being positioned to the west, and located beneath a massive overhanging rock, about thirty feet in

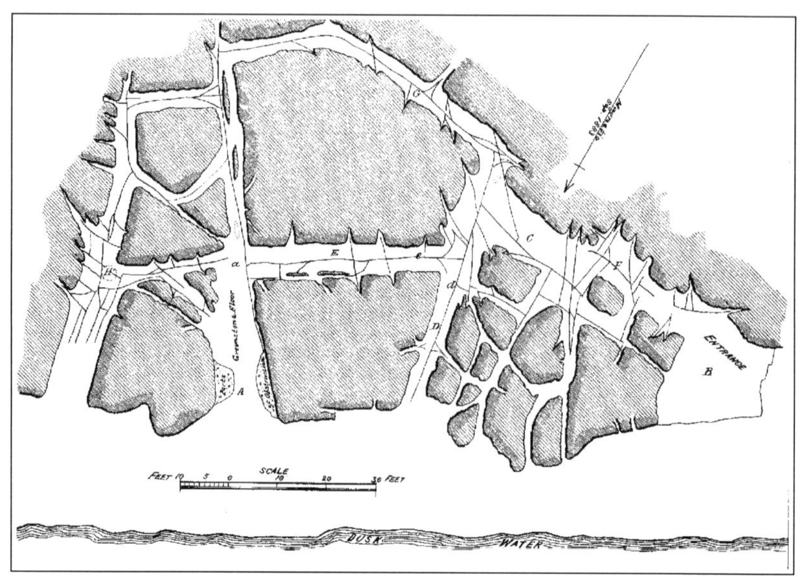

6.1 Cleeves Cove, near Dalry, is an extensive cavern that was used by the Covenanters as well as the fairies. *(Author's Collection)*

height. Within is a complex of caverns measuring 183 feet from the entrance to the innermost part, the width of the cave varying from five to twelve feet. Around the centre the cave opens out into a large cavern, thirty-five feet in length, and rising to twelve feet in height, often described as being like a Gothic arch. A variety of lesser tunnels diverge from this cavern, which is covered with a variety of stalactites. This cave used to be associated with elves, and locals formerly called it the Elf House. In later years it was associated with the Covenanters, who used it as a hiding place from the dragoons.

An old tale associated with Craufurdland Castle, which stands to the north-east of Kilmarnock, recounts how a pot of gold was supposedly lost in a deep pool in the Craufurdland Water, below the ancient castle. The tale of this gold attracted many bounty hunters, but one day, around three hundred years ago, the laird of the castle decided that he would attempt to recover the gold once and for all. He gathered together all the estate workers and they set about building a dam across the river. When they had successfully stopped the water from entering the pool, the estate workers then began bailing the water out of the pool using a chain of buckets. The task was making good progress, and the water was almost emptied when a brownie, or kelpie, yelled from the banking that the castle was on fire. The group sprang up and ran back to the castle where they expected to find it aflame. When they got there the castle was as they left it, perfectly safe. On their return to the stream they discovered that their dam had by this time burst, and the river had refilled the pool with water. Sensing that the brownie's warning was the act of some supernatural guard over the gold, they decided to give up the quest, and the gold has remained safely at the bottom of the pool ever since.

Tradition claims that the fairies were wont to frequent the rocky hillock known as Duniewick, which is located on the north side of Knockdolian, a most wonderful hill on the side of the River Stinchar. Duniewick, or Dunniwick as it was formerly spelled, is in fact the site of a prehistoric hill fort, probably dating from the Bronze Age, though this is unclear. Locals claimed that fairies dance on its rounded summit during the moonlight.

A low hill between Maybole and Dalrymple is known as Downan or Dowan's Hill. Although only 443 feet in height, the summit affords a wide panorama of the district and was used by prehistoric man who built a hill fort there. Local tradition claims that the hill, and Dunree fort, were the haunt of fairies, referred to by Robert Burns in his poem, 'Hallowe'en':

> Upon that night, when fairies light
> On Cassillis Downans dance,
> Or owre the lays, in splendid blaze,
> On sprightly coursers prance.

Downans is an old Scots word that describes green hillocks. Probably most downans were associated with fairies, being like mounds under which the fairies lived. In many places small rounded hills were either named downans or else Fairy Knowe, and these names survive across the county. One example is the south-east of Barr, in the Carrick uplands. The Fairy Knowe there is located in the Water of Gregg glen, the shape of it and the different foliage making it stand out from other hillocks in the area.

Another Fairy Knowe is located near to the village of Kirkmichael, although Catherine Czerkawska claims that it was not named after any fairies, but from the Gaelic *faire* which means watch or guard hill.

Fairy rings or circles were often pointed out by country folk in the past. These could take various forms, from a circle of toadstools or mushrooms, to rings of stones, either set by man or natural. At Lugar, the Rocking Stone at the mouth of the Bello Path, was also referred to by locals as the Fairy Ring, perhaps indicating that strange structures that people could not explain, but recognised that they were not natural, were perhaps the work of the fairies.

Near to the Brickrow Holdings, between Mossblown and Whitletts, east of Ayr, was a circular pool of water known as the Fairy Well. Shown on large scale maps of the nineteenth century, the Fairy Well was a donut-shaped pool, the large diameter of which was 400 feet, the circular island within it being 150 feet in diameter. How it was formed or what tales were associated with it are unknown.

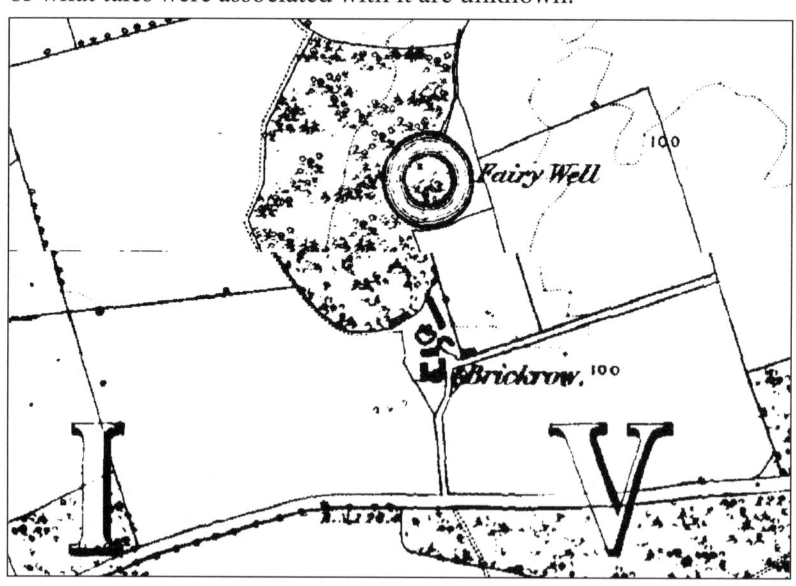

6.2 The Fairy Well, at Brickrow near Mossblown, is a strange circular pool. *(Author's Collection)*

It is said that the fairies were responsible for deciding where the present Cassillis Castle was to be built, the laird originally proposing that his tower should stand on the summit of Dunree. The masons worked hard during the day, cutting and dressing stone for the tower, but at night, when they had returned home and all was dark, the fairies appeared and moved their stones from the hill down into the valley, leaving them on a spot next to the River Doon. The next day the masons made more stones, and laid them for foundations, but again that night the fairies removed them and left them at the same spot adjacent to the Doon. After a few nights of this the laird took the hint, and had Cassillis tower built in the valley, where it stands to this day, seat of the chief of the Kennedys. Similar stories account for the locations of other buildings in Scotland, including St Oran's Chapel on Iona and Ballindalloch Castle in Banffshire.

In Largs there was an old tradition in the town that the fairies used to gather around the 'Tron Tree' during the early hours of the morning. The tron tree was the frame for the public weighing machine, at one time located at Tron Place, near the junction of Aitken and Main streets. During the day the local worthies often gathered around the base of the tron to talk about the goings on in the town. When the public tron was no longer required someone cut it down. The fairies are supposed to

6.3 The fairies were supposed to appear at the Tron Tree in Largs, which was located in Tron Place. *(Dane Love)*

have been so incensed at this, that they caused the death of the culprit's prize sow, for it was found dead on the following day.

There is a traditional tale associated with one of the Kennedys of Culzean, who fought at Flanders in the fourteenth century. One day a very small boy arrived at the castle gate, carrying a wooden pitcher. The tiny boy met the laird as he was leaving and he begged him to give him some ale for his mother, who was sick at the time and was unable to look after herself. The laird took pity on the lad, and informed him to go to the castle and tell the butler that he was to fill up his container from the barrel in the kitchen. The little lad did as he was told, and knocked at the castle door. The butler came and he listened to the story that the lad repeated.

In the kitchen, the butler told the kitchen maid to fill the little lad's pitcher from a barrel of ale that was half full. The maid took it, and began to fill it from the barrel. However, she soon discovered that the barrel had run dry, and the pitcher was only half filled. She told the butler of the situation, and of the fact that the barrel had been half full when she started. The butler told her to open another, for his master had ordered that he fill the lad's pitcher, and that he would do.

The second barrel was tapped and the valve opened. Hardly a drop issued from it when the pitcher was filled. The little lad thanked the butler and the maid for their kindness and went off.

A number of years' later the laird had been captured in Flanders, whilst he was acting as a spy during the war. He was taken to a prison and was sentenced to die on the gallows. On the night before he was due to die he suddenly found the cell door swung open, and the same little lad, whom he now realised was a fairy or elf, shouted:

Laird o' Co',
Rise an' go.

'Co" was a reference to the older name of Culzean Castle – Cove or Coif Castle. The laird jumped up from the bed in the cell and ran out of the prison. The elf grabbed him and threw him up onto his shoulders and ran with him to safety. Indeed, the elf ran so fast that when he let him down he was back at the gate leading to the grounds of Culzean, the very place where they had first met. The elf then spoke to him:

> Ane guid turn deserves anither –
> Tak' ye that for bein' sae kind tae my auld mither.

At that the elf vanished, never to be seen again.

Many of the witchcraft trials of the sixteenth and seventeenth centuries make considerable reference to the witches having consulted fairies, or else having visited the home of the fairies. The case of Bessie Dunlop, the witch of Dalry (in 1576), of which more is told in the chapter on witches, is one of these. At the trial, which was recorded in considerable detail, reference to Bessie having met fairies is given. Apparently she met a spirit on a regular basis, and it was responsible for introducing her to the strange and magical world of 'elf-hame', or the fairy underworld. During the trial reference is made to her meeting with the 'queen of fairy' and her land.

The Queen of Elfhame first appeared to her whilst she lay ill with child in bed. The queen asked her for a drink, and Bessie gave her it. To thank her, the queen predicted Bessie's future. She told her that her child would die, but that her husband, who was also ill, would survive. The queen of the fairies then sent a spirit to assist Bessie – he was Thomas Reid, who had died some time beforehand.

Tom Reid taught Bessie various potions that were useful in treating various ailments in humans and animals. She was also able to summon him to help her solve problems, such as locating things that had become lost or stolen. Her reputation was such that a number of distinguished landowners's wives called on her for assistance, such as Lady Blackhalls, Lady Blair, Lady Johnstone and Lady Kilbowie

On one occasion, Bessie Dunlop was in the vicinity of Leith, near Edinburgh, having travelled there with her husband. It was there that she came upon the fairies, and it was recorded how she was to meet them:

> She had gone afield with her husband to Leith, for home-bringing of meal, and ganging afield to tether her nag at Restalrig Loch, where there came a company of riders by, that made sic a din as heaven and earth had gone together; and incontinent, they rode in to the loch, with many hideous rumble. But Thom[as Reid] told, 'It was the gude wychtis' [good fairies] that were riding in Middle earth.

Bessie is also noted as having met with fairies at an old hawthorn tree, described as the 'Thorne of Damwstarnock' in the account of the trial.

On another occasion she met with the laird of Auchenskeigh at a thorn tree near to Monkcastle. It was at Monkcastle that Bessie Dunlop's associate, Tom Reid, made his way from her. She noted that he 'went away fra' me, in throw the yard at Monkcastell; and I thocht he gait in at ane narroware hoill of the dyke nor ony erdlie [earthly] man culd haif gane throw'. This fact that Reid was able to pass through a tiny hole in a stone dike was seen as being evidence that his spirit appeared to Dunlop as a fairy, and was perhaps passing back to fairyland when he disappeared.

In Bessie's confession there is a reference to her having gone with Tom Reid to Fairlyland. One day, at mid-day, he took her to meet twelve other fairies. These were eight women and four men, and they were instroduced to her as 'gude wychtis that wynnit in the Court of Elfame.'

As time passed, the fairies appear to have requested that Bessie Graham should join them permanently. On one occasion a 'hiddeous uglie sowche of wind followit thame', causing her to feel sick. Reid appeared, and asked her to join them, for he was able to give her a better life in elfhame. All she had to do was deny her Christianity, 'and the faith sche tuke at the funt-stane.' Bessie refused the offer, telling him that 'sche duelt with her awin husband and bairnis' and would not leave them behind. Reid became angry at her refusal to join him, and threatened that he would not help her in the future. Perhaps the withdrawal of Reid's care caused Dunlop to be tried for witchcraft, which occurred in 1576.

Similarly, when John Stewart was tried in Irvine in 1618 on suspect of being a warlock or male witch, reference to fairy belief is mentioned in the case. He is reputed to have regularly met the fairies on the summits of Kilmaurs Hill, as well as Lanark Hill.

Fairies came in different guises, but the friendliest were those known as 'brownies'. Brownies were great assistants, for they would appear at nightfall and carry out some work which was due to be undertaken the following day, so that when one woke up the next morning the task was already completed. Chores such as churning butter, thrashing corn or milling grain were regularly completed by these little folk, who seemed to enjoy work.

Barshare farm at Cumnock was one which had regular assistance from the brownies. Indeed, it had an enviable reputation for being protected by 'the little people'. It was said that for their labour, all they asked in return was a little food, which the farmer left for them in the byre or dairy. It was claimed that a woman who lived at Barshare in the first half of the nineteenth century actually saw these fairies, but she came to no harm.

For a coastal county, Ayrshire has few references to legends associating it with mermaids. These mythical creatures are said to be part female, part fish, and often lured seamen or fishermen onto the rocks and death. Ayrshire's mermaid legend, however, is associated with a 'freshwater mermaid'.

This ancient story associates Knockdolian Castle, near Colmonell, with a mermaid who lived in the River Stinchar. The old tower, which

6.4 Knockdolian Castle, near Colmonell, has associations with the tale of a mermaid. *(Dane Love)*

still stands roofless near to the more modern mansion of 1842, was erected sometime in the sixteenth century, no doubt to replace an even earlier castle. Historically Knockdolian was a seat of the Graham family, but it has passed through a number of hands over the centuries, and tradition ascribes this to the mermaid. At night, when the lady of the castle had put her young son to bed in the upper bedroom of the castle, the mermaid would make its way from the river and perch on a large stone that was black in colour, and quite distinct from the others. During the night she would sit there, singing as she combed her long flowing hair. The singing, however, kept the young child from sleeping, and this greatly annoyed the lady of the house. At length she ordered some estate workers to have the stone broken into pieces, and scattered in the river. That night the mermaid arrived at the usual time, but discovered her perch missing. She began to sing a sombre lullaby:

> Ye may think on your cradle – I'll think on my stane;
> And there'll never be an heir to Knockdolian again.

The lady heard the song, and ran up to the bedroom to look after her son. However, on entering the room she found that the cradle had overturned and that the child lay motionless under it – dead. She and her husband had no more children after that, and the male line of the family died out. The castle and estate passed through the female line, and it seems to have done this a couple of times since.

CHAPTER SEVEN

THE DE'IL

In Ayrshire the Devil is often referred to as 'The De'il', and a number of places are thus shown on the maps. One of the more notable is the De'il's Elbow, a sharp bend on a hill road that links Crosshill with the Balloch. Just over three miles south of Crosshill the minor road makes a quick turn to cross a tributary of the Shiel Burn. There are no known reasons for associating the bend with the devil, and it probably just got its name like the Devil's Elbow in Glenshee from the shape of the road.

At the head of the Glenmuir Water, in the parish of Auchinleck, can be found Connor Linn, a waterfall of some height in a narrow rocky gully. Connor Linn is the name it appears by on the Ordnance Survey map, but locally it is better known as the De'il's Back Door.

The devil has been credited in old legends for the creation of a variety of natural landforms in the county. To the north of Lendalfoot, on Carrick shore, is the Ardmillan Cave, and just above it is the natural rock arch known as the Hole in the Rock. Although natural, locals long claimed that this was created by the devil. One day he was in the act of piling up stones to form sea stacks, when he spotted someone approaching from the south. On closer inspection this turned out to be the minister of Colmonell, and he was armed with his Bible. The devil could not face up to this, so he ran at speed to get away. However, so desperate was his escape that he battered through part of the cliff, leaving the aforementioned hole. The two sea stacks that he had created can still be seen.

The Hole in the Rock and the other rock pillars are geologically explained as former rock headlands and natural arches created by the action of the waves. At one time the water level was higher, but as the ice cap that covered Scotland began to melt, the land raised itself slowly from the sea, leaving what is termed a raised beach, the present flat fields between the current shore and the old cliff life, a few hundred yards or so inland.

7.1 The Hole in the Rock, near Lendalfoot, is said to have been made by the Devil. *(Author's Collection)*

Similarly, it was at one time said that the natural straight lines on the rocks at Craigskelly, on the coast south of Girvan, were the result of the devil wearing out grooves with the wheel of his barrow. Geologists explain the grooves as being the junction of conglomerates with the schists.

A similar story is often told of the Devil making his way to the Island of Arran. Apparently the De'il is gigantic in size, and his large strides across West Kilbride parish took him from one hilltop to another. Local tradition in the area claims that his steps were from Knock Jargon to Tarbet Hill, to Campbelton Hill, to the Ardneil Hill, and then onto Little Cumbrae. At each hilltop his cloven foot left behind scrapes in the rocks, marks that were long pointed out from father to son through the centuries.

A tale of the Devil at Portencross was also popular at one time. Apparently The Old De'il and his son, 'Young Nick' decided to erect two castles across the stretch of firth that separates the island from the mainland. The Old De'il worked at Portencross, whereas his young son built Little Cumbrae Castle. Unfortunately, they only had one hammer between them, and at regular intervals they had to throw this across the water to each other. One of the throws went awry, however, and the hammer landed in the sea, resulting in the castles remaining unfinished thereafter.

A variation of this legend has the two de'ils working away at their castles. The young devil was finished first, whereupon his father set him the task of building a bridge to link Great Cumbrae with the mainland. He erected sizeable foundations on either side of the channel, and was about to commence work on the arch when his father came to inspect the work. The auld de'il was dissatisfied with the workmanship, so he kicked the foundations to bits. This story was used to explain the hole in the Lion Rock on the island.

The Devil is also used to explain an anomaly in the boundaries of Ayrshire parishes. A look at older maps that depict parish boundaries will elicit the fact that the island of Ailsa Craig, located ten miles off the shore at Girvan, is part of the parish of Dailly. However, the remainder of Dailly parish is totally landlocked, and has no coastline whatsoever.

7.2 Ailsa Craig is said to have been a massive lump of rock thrown by the De'il from Dailly parish into the Firth of Clyde. *(Author's Collection)*

In fact, the nearest part of Dailly parish to the sea is at Laigh Killoup, fully one and a half miles from the sea. The shore in this vicinity is either in the parish of Girvan, or else Kirkoswald, north of the Curragh.

Old stories claim that the Devil was making his way across Carrick and in some fit of temper grabbed a large chunk of hillside, usually claimed to be part of Maxwellston or Hadyard Hill, and threw it into the Firth of Clyde. This resulted in Ailsa Craig being created, and as it came from Dailly parish it was to remain in Dailly parish. The hollow created on the side of Maxwellston Hill is said to be the glen where the Penwhapple Reservoir now lies.

In these modern less superstitious times, we don't need to disprove this tale, but of course the rock in both places is totally different, Ailsa Craig being comprised of granite, famed for its use in curling stones, whereas Maxwellston Hill is made from totally different rocks. However, we need to try to explain why Ailsa Craig is part of Dailly parish, and not part of either Girvan or Kirkoswald. The reason is that the island was regarded as being part of the Barony of Knockgerran, which place lies within Dailly parish. Knockgerran, and thus the island, were the property of the Marquis of Ailsa, who took his title from it.

Another old tradition associates Ailsa Craig with Ireland. Today the island is often referred to as 'Paddy's Milestone' being midway between Glasgow and Belfast, and thus marks the half way point on journeys by sea between the two cities. However, older tradition claims that Ailsa Craig was part of the kingdom of Ireland, rather than Scotland. Apparently an Irish king, named King Brian Boroimhe, laid claim to the island sometime around the year 1000. Old Irish tradition uses this tale to explain the fact that as there are no snakes on Ailsa Craig, it must be part of Ireland, there being no snakes there, traditionally being banished from the island by St Patrick. According to Irish legends, Ailsa Craig is known to them as 'Brian's Stone'.

A number of Ayrshire folk have been associated with the Devil over the centuries. Often the link came about as a result of that person's good luck, or else because of their ill-luck, such was the wont of the locals to tell tales and elaborate them as they passed from mouth to mouth. A case in point was a land-owner in the Ardrossan area, named Sir Fergus Barclay. He was rather fond of betting, and was renowned for his love of the horse-race. So keen was he that he even travelled around Europe, betting at races and other events. Indeed, it became the case that many people refused to bet against him, so certain were the odds for the horses he selected. Such was Barclay's good luck that the residents of Ardrossan began to suspect that there was something behind his skill in picking winners, and soon had him in legion with the Devil. Indeed, so linked with the Devil did Sir Fergus supposedly become, that he was given the nick-name, the De'il of Ardrossan. It was reckoned that his horse's bridle, which we can assume was rather finer than that customarily used at the time, was his secret charm, and that he had obtained it in a pact with the devil. Various versions of this story have been told, not only in the Ardrossan area, but around Britain, where numerous tales associate folk having sold their soul to the devil in return for earthly favours.

The De'il of Ardrossan is traditionally said to have been interred in the old kirkyard that lies on the town's Castle Hill. A local legend claims that if one took some soil from the sorcerer's grave and threw it into the sea, then a massive storm or tempest would start almost immediately, often with disastrous consequences.

At one time the last laird of Fail Castle was known as the 'Warlock' from the tricks he played on locals. Who the laird was is unconfirmed, but it may have been Walter Whiteford. A great storm blew across Ayrshire on the day of his funeral. When his corpse was carried out of the tower house in his coffin, the winds became so great that they blew the roof off. From that time onwards the castle remained in ruins, gradually decaying until 1952, when the last remaining walls were demolished and the stones used to provide bottoming for Prestwick Airport runway! Some stones, however, were used to form a grotto in the grounds of the chapel at Annbank.

The story of the Warlock of Fail was recounted in verse by Joseph Train, a local historian and correspondent of Sir Walter Scott. Train was born in Sorn, but moved to Galloway and lived near Castle Douglas. In *Strains of the Mountain Muse*, published in 1814, Strain includes a ballad entitled 'The Warlock Laird'.

One of the warlock's tricks is recounted as follows. One day, the men of a farm were working in the fields and the gudewife was at home, preparing their supper. As she worked, the warlock of Fail knocked at the door and asked for a drink. The wife refused, being too busy to supply refreshments to passing travellers. The warlock then took from his bag a 'merry pin', which was some form of magic stick. He pushed it into the thatch over the front door of the cottage and stood back to watch. Within, the lady of the house left her chores and began to dance and sing in the middle of the floor. This she kept up for hours, ignoring the fact that she had been busily preparing supper.

Time passed slowly for the workers in the fields, and their hunger was growing ever more stronger. Eventually they realised that suppertime must have passed, and one by one they gradually drifted to the cot-house, to see what had happened to their meal. As the first passed under the 'merry pin' and entered the cottage he was greeted by the dancing wife. About to berate her for enjoying herself and not preparing food for the workers, he was overcome by some magic and immediately joined in the dance.

As time passed again, a second worker decided to go to the cottage and investigate. As he, too, passed under the 'merry pin' he felt the urge to join in the fun, and soon was dancing and singing with the rest. Eventually all of the men from the fields were dancing reels and jigs in the small cottage. The warlock let them do this for some time before he walked to the front door. As soon as he removed the 'merry pin' the occupants fell to the floor, totally exhausted, and unable to rise for some time.

Another warlock whose existence and actions were at one time popular was the warlock of Innermessan. Although not an Ayrshire place – Innermessan is the name of a small clachan and lost village near to the head of Loch Ryan in Wigtownshire – the warlock has an association with Ballantrae, in the county. By day the warlock, named Peter, worked as a boat builder, and he was asked by some local fishermen at Ballantrae to build them a new boat. Peter was skilled at this, and commenced work on the vessel. As he was busily shaping boards to fit onto the ribs of the boat he was watched by many villagers, impressed at his skill. As they spectated, one of them spotted someone travelling at great speed down the road to the south of Ballantrae. His horse was galloping at a fast pace, and the rider pushed him ever faster.

'That laddie's traivelin' rather hot foot,' exclaimed one of the onlookers.

'Does he?' asked Peter, 'he'll jist bide there a bit.'

Casting a spell on the rider, as he made his way into the River Stinchar his horse froze in mid gallop. The hind legs were still in the water, but the fore legs were stopped in mid air. The rider was held in pose and both he and his horse were as still as a statue. Peter went back to his work, fashioning timbers to suit the boat, ignoring the onlookers as they laughed at the rider still frozen to the spot. As he worked, the warlock uttered the words, 'Gang yer gait!' at which point the horse and rider continued on as if nothing had happened.

The people of Ballantrae are said to have thought that the vessel that Peter was making would have some form of spiritual luck that no other fishing boat would have, and were marvelling at the thought. However, once Peter had been paid, and as he left to walk back through Glen App to Innermessan, he commented, 'That boat will droon her fu.' The Ballantrae fishermen ignored the comment for some time, delighted at having such a well-made craft. However, it is said that one totally calm day, when the boat was making its way back into the tiny harbour at the village foreland, a sudden squall blew up and the boat was forced back out into the middle of the firth. As nightfall was approaching, no assistance could be offered, and the boat and its crew were never seen again.

There are a number of traditional tales that associate things with the devil. One of the oldest stories, reportedly recounted in an early book of tales, gives the story of the 'De'il of Prestwick'. This story may have been a popular fireside tale that was recounted across the country, but certainly one account claims that it happened in Prestwick.

It is said that sometime near the end of the seventeenth century, when folk were far more superstitious that they hitherto were, a young lad was committing a regular series of nuisances in the burgh, much to the annoyance of the inhabitants. On one occasion he made his way into a field belonging to one of the magistrates, and there he destroyed much of his crop of pease. The delinquent was caught, and he was taken to the tolbooth in the town and there locked up. His friend, David Rankine, who is said to have been a blacksmith in Kilmarnock at a later date, managed to obtain the key for the cell from the lock-keeper whilst he was sleeping. He made his way to the lock-up and let his friend go. The two spotted a stirk, or young cow, in a field nearby, so they caught it and managed to place it in the cell. Once the door was locked again they returned the key to its rightful place, all the time the gaoler being fast asleep.

On the following morning, at about ten o'clock, the time when the lad was supposed to be called before the court, the magistrates discovered that the cell contained the stirk, which by this time was bellowing in hunger. The magistrates were rather superstitious, and immediately thought that this was the devil himself, in the guise of a stirk, and he had eaten the prisoner. As far as they were concerned, he was bellowing in search of more food. Accordingly, they ran off for their own safety.

The magistrates decided that they would have to call the minister, in order that he could 'lay' the devil. David Rankine offered to run for him, and when he arrived at the manse he explained how he and his friend had hoodwinked the magistrates. The minister must have laughed at how silly the officials were, and he agreed to return with Rankine to 'lay the de'il'. The stirk was safely removed, and the miscreant reappeared, totally unharmed. The magistrates were so relieved to find the devil removed and their prisoner unharmed that they decided that he had suffered enough and let him go.

According to the old account of this tale, David Rankine carried out a similar prank on the parishioners of St Quivox. During the night he caught the minister's cow and he led it into the kirkyard. Up against the gable of the old church he found the rope that rung the kirk bell. He tied this rope to the tail of the cow and left him there. The cow, naturally, began to move around, and when he had wandered far enough, its tail tugged at the kirk bell, ringing it. The cow became alarmed at the sound, as well as the fact that it was tied up, and began to move more erratically, causing the bell to ring more. The cow started to bellow, and the St Quivox villagers were woken during the night by the sound. Some lifted lanterns and made their way into the kirkyard, only to see Beelzebub himself in the kirkyard, ringing the bell irregularly. The truth was not discovered until the morning, when daylight revealed the truth.

A traditional tale associates the Devil with Rowallan Castle, north of Kilmarnock. One night the laird was having a party, one that many of the locals were invited to. The party was in full swing, and everyone was enjoying themselves in the great hall of the castle, merry-making and feasting. The devil came to hear about the festivities, and was incensed that he had not been invited. With his wife, a witch, he made his way to Rowallan. Outside, in the courtyard in front of the castle, they stopped, and listened to the partying within. Angrier than ever, he made his way up the stairs and opened the main door. There he was met by the local minister, who had been invited. Taken aback at who had greeted him on entering, the devil stopped. The minister recognised the devil, and yelled out, 'Avaunt thou, in the name of God!' At the same time he hit the devil on the head, between his horns, with his Bible. The devil turned around quickly, and ran out of the door once more, his cloven hooves battering down the steps. Visitors to Rowallan Castle from that time onward often looked at the steps to find the stone that had been cracked by the devil's hoofprints as he legged it. Archibald Adamson, writing in 1875, noted that at that time the step was still rent, although he pointed out that it was best seen in wet weather.

7.3 The De'il was not invited to a party at Rowallan Castle, north of Kilmarnock, and caused a crack in the tread of the impressive stairway. *(Will Morton)*

An old account claims that the devil made night-time appearances at Mansfield, to the east of New Cumnock. An old mill, which has a reputation of being haunted, as well as a couple of farms of the name, gather around the site of an old mansion, for a number of years the seat of the Stuart-Menteth family. According to Helen Steven, writing in

1899, the devil 'feared the folk at Mansfield Barn with a loud noise like running waters, and a low, rough sound like the grating of a water-wheel. But when they looked, the wheel had never stirred; and it was no wind that sighed and moaned round the house on the still, starry nights and shrieked in at the doors and windows.' It was also reported that in the morning cloven foot-prints could be seen in the yard of the steading, and yet no cloven-footed animal had been there during the night. 'Who or what could it be but the arch-enemy himself!' she wrote.

Also in the parish of New Cumnock, but at the western end, stand the fragmentary ruins of Waterhead Castle. Little today other than a low mound marks where a stronghold once stood, the walls long having crumbled into the ground and become overgrown. However, at one time the ruins were more extensive than they are today, with walls, windows and old chimneys still in existence. The ruins were claimed to have been the haunt of the devil. Locals claimed that on some nights when they looked at the ruins it appeared as though the windows were lit, smoke bellowed from the chimneys, and the sound of screeching and laughter echoed from within. It was also pointed out by old farmers, who believed in such matters, that the cattle could see or feel more than humans could, and on such nights they gave the old castle a wide berth. Should they be driven towards the castle, then they became restless, their eyes becoming bloodshot, and they fought with each other.

In early times, when the country folk of the county were more suspicious of new methods being introduced, they often associated them with the devil. Thus, in the early eighteenth century, agricultural labourers and farmers named the new fangled method of winnowing corn and other grain crops as using the 'De'il's Wind.' The traditional method was to lift a basketful of grain in a flattish container, throw the grain up into the air, the wind blowing the chaff and other impurities away, the heavy grain falling back into the tray. When the new winnowing machines were invented and brought into the county the artificial wind created was classed as being the work of the de'il, and not the natural wind supplied by God. It was noted that even some ministers exhorted from the pulpit that the farmers should desist from using the 'De'il's wind'.

An old traditional tale from Carrick associates the devil with the Earl of Cassillis. Gilbert Kennedy, the second earl, was the person whom

7.4 The gravestone of Gilbert MacAdam at Kirkmichael, who was shot by the laird of Culzean, resulting in Culzean's soul being claimed by the Devil. *(Author's Collection)*

tradition claims roasted the abbot of Crossraguel Abbey in the black vault of Dunure Castle, in order to torture him into handing over the title to various lands in Carrick. Locals always associated him with the devil, and it was said that at the time while he was torturing the abbot a black raven was never far from his person. This raven was said to be the incarnation of the devil himself, and he was there to advise Kennedy on what to do. Gilbert Kennedy was to suffer himself, for he was murdered at Prestwick in 1527.

A popular tale recounts that on the night that Kennedy was murdered, a fisherman in the firth near to Ailsa Craig was looking out over the waves when he saw an eery sight. At first he was not fully aware of what he saw, but on studying the image closely realised that it was a fiery chariot, being drawn by a number of horses, their manes aflame. The apparition of fire passed relatively close to the fishing boat.

With a bravery beyond the norm, he yelled across the waters to the driver of the coach, 'From Whence to where?'

'From Hell to Culzean's burial,' was the reply. 'I have come to collect the earl's soul.'

The fisherman was still pondering what he had witnessed when he saw the carriage making a high-speed return journey. He didn't shout on this occasion, but he could see the earl tied to the back of the carriage, writhing around in agony, trying to escape.

A further tradition regarding the earl's funeral was that when the funeral cortege left Dunure Castle, the coffin located on the back of a horse-drawn hearse, a black raven appeared as if by magic from the sky and perched on the coffin. The mourners were too scared to frighten it away, for they all recognised the symbolism of the bird as a bad omen. It is said that the horses that were pulling the bier refused to budge until the bird had flown from the coffin. The party then made their way from Dunure to the Collegiate Church in Maybole, where the earl was to be buried, the raven flying over them at a fairly close distance.

The story of the earl and the devil claiming his soul has also been attributed to Sir Archibald Kennedy of Culzean, who was a persecutor of the Covenanters. The gravestone to Gilbert MacAdam at Kirkmichael notes that he 'was shot in this parish by the Laird of Colzean and Ballochmil' for his Covenanting adherences in 1685. After the Glorious Revolution, Kennedy and Reid of Ballochmyle did not wish their persecutions to be recorded on stone and had their names obliterated. However, their names were cut even deeper into the stone again, perhaps by Robert Paterson, the original of Sir Walter Scott's *Old Mortality*. Kennedy died in 1710, and the tale of the Devil claiming his soul became common once more.

An old story popular in the Carrick area connects the De'il with the laird of Changue, a small upland estate near to the village of Barr. The laird was losing quite a bit of money, tradition does not state how, but he soon found himself in considerable debt. The Devil appeared to him one day and offered to buy his soul for what was a princely sum – a figure that would both clear Changue's debt and give him sufficient funds to live the life of Reilly for the next year. Changue agreed to the sale, and with the funds given to him by the Devil was able to pay off his debts and enjoy life once more. Time passed, and the following year the Devil returned to Changue, ready to collect his dues by taking the soul of his debtor, and the body of the laird to hell. The laird had changed his mind by this time, and was unwilling to give in without a fight. The Devil lunged at Changue, trying to grab hold of him. However, the laird was wise, and was quick enough to place his Bible on the ground between them, preventing the Devil from passing over it. The laird then took his sword and inscribed a circle on the ground round about him, including the Bible within the circle. The Devil was unable to pass over the circle, and the laird was able to stay within the mark long enough for him to dour out the Devil. At length, Satan left the spot and returned to Hell – alone.

The place where the laird of Change fended off the Devil was for many years pointed out on the ground. It was located on a low knoll known as Craiganrarie, or Craigenrery as it is shown on current maps, just twelve hundred yards north of High Changue farm. On the ground a circle, only four and a half feet in diameter, could be seen, as well as the mark left on the ground by the Bible and the two footprints of the laird.

CHAPTER EIGHT

SAINTS and MIRACLES

A number of early saints are associated with Ayrshire. Some may have lived for a time in what became the county, others may have just passed through, whereas others may simply be commemorated by having churches or other places dedicated to their memory.

The Manor Park Hotel, located on a high bluff between Largs and Skelmorlie, was originally known as St Fillan's House. The present building dates from 1843 but it occupies a much older site. There are a couple of places in the immediate area that are supposed to have connections with St Fillan, who was a Scoto-Irish saint, and who is reputed to have died in the year 649. St Fillan is today more associated with Perthshire, where numerous relics and places associated with him can be found, including a village named after him.

At the Manor Park Hotel was an old well, located near to the wall of the enclosed garden, which is traditionally known as St Fillan's Well. It is said that a chapel dedicated to St Fillan also existed hereabouts, but its site can no longer be discerned on the ground.

St Inan is associated with a number of locations in northern Ayrshire. The town of Irvine has a number of connections with this saint, who is said to have lived in the late eighth and early ninth century. He was sometimes named St Evan and lived in Irvine for a time. He is supposed to have predicted the victory of King Kenneth MacAlpin of the Scots over the Picts, thus creating a united Scotland for the first time. In Irvine there was at one time a well in Harbour Street that was named in honour of the saint, and for many years after the well had gone, a building known as St Inan's survived. Some say that St Inan managed to visit Rome and Jerusalem, but this may just be fanciful speculation. St Inan is thought to have died on 18 August 839 and some traditions claim that he was buried in Irvine.

Other places that have connections with St Inan include the former estate of Southannan near Fairlie, in the parish of West Kilbride. As there is no 'Northannan' it is claimed that the name is derived from St Inan. Lord Semple, who owned that castle that stood there, also restored the chapel in Fairlie and had it dedicated to St Inan. In Dundonald Castle there was a chapel dedicated to St Inan, and many years ago a chaplain received an endowment to perform divine service within it.

Beith is another community associated with St Inan. The village's traditional fair was known as Tenant's Day, which is a corruption of Tinnan's or St Inan's Day. This was always held on 18 August, the date of the saint's death.

To the east of Beith, on the slopes of Lochlands Hill, can still be found St Inan's Well and St Inan's Chair. The latter is a cleft in the cliff-face which has two rock buttresses located on either side of a low seat, which in recent years has been refashioned in concrete. The buttresses lean over the seat, almost like a gothic arch, protecting the sitter from

8.1 St Inan's Chair is a sheltered hollow in the natural cliff face, east of Beith. *(Dane Love)*

8.2 St Inan's Well still flows at the foot of Lochlands Hill, east of Beith. *(Dane Love)*

the winds. The saint is supposed to have sat and conducted services from here, but the congregation would have had to be arranged far down the hill below, there being no convenient place where to stand. More likely, the seat would have been used by the saint as a place of solitary reflection. Near to the seat is the well, which is noted as being always full of fresh clear water. The well has been lined with stone and covered with flat stones. From this chamber a pipe takes the water to the side of the road.

The town of Kilwinning is named in honour of St Winning, said to have been an Irish missionary who arrived in Scotland sometime in the second half of the seventh century. He travelled through the west of Scotland, converting the locals to Christianity, or at least extending the works commenced by St Ninian three and a half centuries earlier. St Winning is thought to be the same person as St Finnan, a name more commonly used in the rest of Scotland. St Winning is said to have died in the year 715. For centuries his feast day or festival was held on 21 January, celebrated in Kilwinning for many centuries.

In Ayrshire a number of places associated with this saint can still be found, the most noted being the steep hill between Dalry and Kilbirnie known as Carwinning Hill. The name derives from 'caer' Winning, or the castle or fort of Winning. The remains of a prehistoric fort do, in fact, crown the flat summit of the hill, which is 650 feet in height and affords a wide panoramic view. A stone battle-axe head and a bronze chisel were found when the fort was excavated in 1977.

8.3 Carwinning Hill, near Dalry, is associated with St Winning. *(Dane Love)*

We have already read about St Winning's Well in Kilwinning and its legend in a previous chapter. Kilwinning Abbey, a Tironensian monastery erected in the late twelfth century, probably occupies the site of either St Winning's cell or an early church dedicated to him. The abbey was dedicated to St Winning and the Virgin Mary.

There are a number of ancient tales associated with St Winning. One claims that the River Garnock had its watercourse redirected by him. Geologists and geographers have discovered that the river at one time did not flow into the River Irvine before the two watercourses made their way to the sea over Irvine Bar, but that the Garnock at one time turned westwards shortly after leaving Kilwinning and made its way past Dubbs and Ardeer House before flowing into the Firth of Clyde below Stevenston. When the river changed route is not fully known, some accounts claiming that it was as recently as four or five centuries ago, whereas the traditional tale claims that it happened sometime in the first few centuries *anno domini.* The tale states that St

Winning, who was based at his cell in Kilwinning, sent some of his servants to the River Garnock to catch some fish for eating. The servants spent most of the day in pursuit of the fish, but were unable to catch any. Dejected, they returned back to the cell and reported back to St Winning. The saint went mad, and in his rage cursed the River Garnock. The river, in trying to avoid the wrath of St Winning, turned its back on the saint and made its way southwards, creating the current watercourse.

The village of Kirkoswald is named in honour of St Oswald, who is said to have fought a battle here. It was the year AD 634, and Oswald, who was a young Northumbrian prince, and his supporters defeated the enemies who had deposed his father. It is said that King Ethelfrith was murdered by an enemy who captured the young Oswald and sent him to Iona in exile. There Oswald is supposed to have been converted to Christianity, and from Iona decided to regain his father's kingdom, as well as converting it to a Christian nation. His supporters grew as he made his way south, and it was on the Carrick plains that he met his enemies. Oswald's supporters gathered to the north of Hallowshean Hill, his opponents to the south. The night before battle, Oswald prayed to God and made a vow that should he win, then he would erect a church to His glory.

Being victorious, St Oswald decided to erect a church on the spot where he had defeated the enemy. A simple building, the church stood for centuries until it was replaced by the masons employed in erecting nearby Crossraguel Abbey in 1244. The present parish church was erected in 1777, since when the old church has become ruinous. Oswald subsequently continued south to Northumbria and regained his throne, becoming King Oswald. He reigned for only eight years, for he was to be killed at the Battle of Maserfelth in AD 642. Within a few years he was canonised as a saint.

By the fifteenth century and later these saints became more associated with the local fair than any ecclesiastical connection. Many churches and chapels organised festivals, or *feria*, hence the word fair, on the saint's day associated with their church. Thus, different villages held their fair at different times of the years, the following table being a selection of those taking place across Ayrshire at one time.

Lammas Fair	Maybole	1 August	
Mary Mass Fair	Irvine	3rd Monday in August	
Midsummer Fair	Ayr	last Tuesday in Hune	*also* St John's Day
St Brennan's Fair	Kilbirnie	May	
St Bride's Fair	West Kilbride	1 February	*also* Bridesday
St Colm's Fair	Largs	2nd Tuesday in June	*also* St Columba's Fair
St Marnock's Fair	Kilmarnock	25 October	
St Matthew's Fair	Old Cumnock	21 September	
St Peter's Fair	Galston	29 June	
St Ternan's Fair	Beith	30 August	*also* Tennan's Day
St Winning's Fair	Kilwinning	2 February	*also* Winning's Day

Miracles

There is an old story that claims that a miracle of God took place in 1775 when the Associate Church in Cumnock was being built by its members. This group of worshippers had established themselves as a congregation in 1773 and was soon thriving sufficiently to consider building their own place of worship. However, there was some difficulty in carrying this through, for the Marquis of Bute was the principal owner in the parish, and he refused to sell them a piece of ground on which to build a church. Indeed, it was said that he placed every obstacle that he could in the way of the congregation. Other landowners in the parish were of a similar feeling, and thus the members could not obtain some ground. At length, however, one John Murdoch in the village had some sympathy for the members and he decided to sell them ten falls of ground at the 'Townfoot of Cumnock' whereon to build a place of worship. The original title deed was drawn up and signed by Gavin Hamilton, the friend of Robert Burns.

Obstacles were still placed in the way of the congregation, for no local quarry was available for their purpose, being mainly in the ownership of Lord Bute or opponents of the church. Undaunted, and at great cost and energy, the congregation managed to obtain stone with which to build the church from a neighbouring parish, which was brought to New Bridge Street. The builders had sufficient sand and lime to commence work on the foundations, but soon they had exhausted their sand supplies and the masons had to abandon the project for some time. It was noted by the congregation that the adjacent Glaisnock Water that flows past the church was at the time rather low and that

8.4 The 'Cumnock Miracle' allowed the congregation to erect the original Associate Church on this site in Cumnock. *(Dane Love)*

plentiful natural sand lay along its banks and in the bed of the watercourse. However, the Marquis of Bute claimed that the banks of the Glaisnock as well as its bed was also his property, and thus if they took sand from there they would be guilty of theft. Writing in 1899, Helen Steven noted that, 'the stoppage of the work for so insignificant a reason was regarded as a huge joke and served as the text for much mirth and idle-speaking.'

According to *Memories of Scottish Scenes and Sabbaths more than Eighty Years Ago*, written by Rev Alexander Kennedy of Ontario, Canada, in 1902, 'in no great time Providence supplied them with abundance of sand without putting them to any trouble or cost, not even the cost of cartage, and by means as little expected by the friends as by the foes of dissent. The Lord sent "a plenteous rain," causing an unusually high flood – in all likelihood a Lammas flood. The two streams, which were united, overflowed their banks, covering the low walls of the arrested building. When the waters subsided it was found that a large quantity of sand brought down by the rushing stream had been deposited within and around the walls – amply sufficient, it was said, to complete the building.'

The strange flood and its consequences were much talked about by the congregation thereafter, as well as by others in the village, so much so that it became known as the 'Cumnock Miracle'.

CHAPTER NINE

WITCHES and WARLOCKS

Scotland in the sixteenth century was a place that feared evil in all its guises. The people of the countryside believed in numerous superstitions, and anything that could not be explained by normal, Christian means were seen to be a sign of the Devil's work. Witches existed almost everywhere, and seem to have done from time immemorial. However, in 1563 the Scottish Parliament issued a law which stated that 'all who used witchcraft, sorcery, necromancy, or pretended skilles therein, and all consulters of witches and sorcerers should be punished capitally.' This formalised and made legal the persecution of those suspected of witchcraft, and the hunt for them began with a vengeance. Even the king, James VI, was afraid of witches, and in 1597 he wrote a book entitled *Daemonologie*, republished in London in 1603. This was to help his subjects to identify witches and wizards and thus bring them to trial.

Unfortunately, many innocent women were to be persecuted for their supposed skills as a witch. In many cases suspected associations with the Devil were used as reasons to get rid of old and unwanted widows, strange women who perhaps today would be classed as mentally ill or disabled in some way. Recent research by Alastair Hendry has uncovered 168 cases of witchcraft in Ayrshire that were tried.

In Dundonald in January 1602 a woman was reported to the kirk session for bewitching a neighbour's cattle, or 'ky' as it is recorded in the minute book. Her case was discussed at length for some years, and no real conclusion came of it. Similarly, Patrick Lowrie, a warlock, and Catherine MacTear, a witch, were tried for their crimes. This lasted for almost five years, but no verdict was forthcoming. However, on 8

November 1629, Rev Robert Ramsay, in Dundonald kirk, 'publictlie out of pulpite, by the authoritie of the Presbytery, did inhibite and discharge all sorte of charming and resorteing to charmers, consulting with wizards, sorcerers and uthers of that sort; certifeing all and sundrie whoe did so in time comeing they sould be challengit criminallie therefore and followed and persewit unto death as for the crime of witchcraft.'

It was reckoned that witches had certain parts of their body where they could feel no pain, and many 'witch-finders' established themselves all over the country. Suspect witches were tied and bound, and these finders began stabbing at their body with a large pin, trying to find some piece of skin where they seemed to experience no pain. In 1644 the Presbytery of Ayr considered employing a professional witchfinder from Galloway.

Suspected witches were reported to the local presbytery, and the ministers would be given the task of deciding whether there was a case to investigate. If they thought there was then she would be reported to the burgh magistrates or local council. The provost and bailies of the burghs would consider whether there was sufficient evidence for a trial, and if they did, then the Kirk session was given permission to apply to the Lords of Council in Edinburgh for a commission to try the woman as a witch.

One of the witches of Cumnock was Nannie Reid, who lived in the early part of the nineteenth century. She does not seem to have been a too evil character, however, for her powers seem to have been limited to causing cows to give little milk, or making scones which were being baked to be of the wrong consistency, or else to burn on the girdle. Many local folk in the town blamed such instances on Nannie Reid, and by way of preventing her from picking on them, would give her small gifts of money or provisions. It was noted that when Nannie Reid was treated well she did no harm.

The folk around Cumnock believed that witches could transform themselves into different animals, in particular hares. One day there was a fairly young lad out shooting on the farm of Lowes, between Old and New Cumnock. He spotted a hare, and shot at it from his gun. He was aware of it being hit full blast with the shot, but the hare seemed to rear up on its hind legs and wag its front paws at him. The friends who were with him warned him that he had shot a witch, and that he would suffer from some major calamity within a few days. The lad was terrified, and found a wise old woman in the district who was able to tell him what to do to prevent the curse from taking place. He was to return to the very spot where he shot the hare, and fire a piece of silver from his gun into the air. Silver was regarded as having anti-satanic powers, and firing it through the air was thought to kill off the witch's spirit.

Another tale associating a witch turning into a hare is recounted in D. C. Cuthbertson's *Carrick Days*, published in 1933. In it he claims that the locals at Ballantrae told him of a local witch that had died in the past year or two, that is, so recently as 1930 or thereabouts. Witches by this time were not persecuted as in the past, but the villagers kept a safe distant from the old woman. She was still reputed to cast spells, and one of the recipients of these was the local minister. She was out gathering sticks on the Sabbath when she died, or at least her earthly body died. The locals became aware that they had not seen the old *cailleach* for some time, so they went to her cottage and had to force open the door. As they did, a hare got up from adjacent to the doorstep and ran towards the hills. The hare was still regarded at that time as being the manifestation of the witch.

At Ochiltree, near to the cemetery on the road towards Mauchline, is a mound known as the Witch Knowe. This earthwork stands above a steep bank down to the Lugar Water, and is protected by a ditch six feet deep on the other sides. It is known to be a Norman motte hill, and what connection there was with witches is unknown. There are a number of other Witch Knowes in the area, though not all were sites of Norman dwellings. Near Townhead of Greenock farm, Muirkirk, is a Witch Knowe, located above the River Ayr. Another is a prehistoric mound located near to Westpark farm, near Coylton. A smallish mound, this was obviously man-made, but for what purpose is not known. At Riccarton in Kilmarnock, Witchknowe was the name of a farm that was formerly located at the junction of the present Witchknowe Road with Bruce Street.

A story associated with the witch of Craigie, near Kilmarnock, explains her connection with a huge boulder which formerly stood outside the village. According to the traditional tale, this witch fell foul of the church, which was planning to have her brought before it and tried. In umbrage, the witch lifted a huge boulder from the hillside which she proposed dropping through the roof of the kirk. She carried the boulder in her apron but, fortunately for the parishioners, the strings on her apron broke and the boulder fell short of its target. It lay in a field just outside the kirkyard for many centuries. The boulder was known as the White Stane, or alternatively Witch's Stone. Later in time the farmer in whose field the stone fell decided that it had become a nuisance to him. He arranged to have it blasted with gunpowder, and the pile of broken stones that resulted needed twenty-five cart-loads to move. Some of the stone is said to have been used in the building of the Craigie Inn. A knoll that forms part of Craigie Hill is still known as the Witch Knowe, and it may have been from there that the boulder was originally plucked.

9.1 Craigie Church, south of Kilmarnock, was the target of a huge boulder supposedly thrown at it by a witch. *(Dane Love)*

Bessie Dunlop, the witch of Dalry, was one of the earlier known witches. In 1576 Elizabeth (known as Bessie) Dunlop, the wife of Andrew Jack in Linn, was called before the High Court, accused of various acts of sorcery and witchcraft, although these seem to be limited to using supernatural methods to locate lost or missing items or to cure various diseases. She was no doubt tortured, and it was her own confession that was the greatest evidence used to find her guilty. Robert Pitcairn noted that this case was one of the most extraordinary on record, due to its 'very minute and graphic detail'.

Dunlop's associations with witchcraft seem to have started when she was driving her cows to pasture. On the way she met with Thomas, or Tom, Reid, who was the factor on Blair estate. Dunlop was sad, there being affliction in her family, but on meeting Reid struck up a friendship. He told her not to worry about her difficulties, and predicted what the outcome of these would be. The only problem was that Tom Reid had been killed at the Battle of Pinkie in 1547, 29 years earlier.

Bessie and Reid became friends thereafter, he often manifesting before her. She described him as being an honest, elderly man, sporting a long grey beard and carrying a white wand. He taught her various tricks and how to make potions, and gradually she began to gain the ability to cure disease and for predicting where stolen goods were hidden. One of her potions involved taking a beetroot, drying it, and grinding it into a powder. This supposedly cured two children and a cow. A second potion had ginger, aniseed, cloves, liquorice and ale mixed together, brought to the boil and sweetened with sugar. A local woman, Lady Johnston, had a daughter who was susceptible to fainting, and this mixture was made for her. She was informed to drink it every morning before taking food. In payment, Bessie received some meal and cheese.

For a time Bessie Dunlop was in great demand in the parish, but soon her mystical ways came to the notice of the authorities. She was apprehended and dragged off to the tollbooth in Irvine, from where she was sent on to Edinburgh for trial. At the trial she confirmed that she had never met Tom Reid during his lifetime, but that he had appeared to her on a number of occasions, including once in Edinburgh's High Street, and another time in the kirkyard of Dalry. During the trial the interrogators tried to get her to renounce her baptism, but Bessie refused to do this. Other notions of what a witch may get up to were placed before her, hoping to obtain a confession from her. 'Had she copulated with Thom Reid?' was asked, but she denied this. Her thoughts on the success and future of the reformation were also inquired of, and whether or not she had any gift of prophecy.

The prophetic skills that were placed against Dunlop were rather mundane, but seemingly enough to help her conviction. She was accused of talking of 'the evill weddir that was to cum', - but almost any Ayrshire man or woman can predict bad weather!

Found guilty of witchcraft, she was sentenced to be 'worried' at the stake, after which she was to be burned to death. Her accomplice, Thomas Reid, tried to intervene on her behalf, but his pleas seem only to have helped find her guilty, as he claimed that her powers were only used to help others, and that they were not used to iniquitous ends. The account of Bessie Dunlop is recorded in Robert Pitcairn's *Ancient Criminal Trials in Scotland 1488-1624*, published in 1833, and Sir Walter Scott refers to her in his essay on *Demonology and Witchcraft*, and yet there seems to have been no local tradition handed down in the Dalry area of her cruel execution.

It was not just women who were tried and executed for witchcraft. Men, who were usually described as warlocks or wizards, were also liable to be taken and tried for dealing with spirits and being in league with the Devil. Research has found that the ratio of witches to warlocks was around 86% female to 14% male. However, treatment in court of those accused appears to be quite similar, around 56% of women, compared to 52% of men, being found guilty once their case got that far. In 1583 there were at least six men who were tried in Ayrshire for being suspect wizards. These were Matthew Bryce, James Campbell, John Richard, Alexander Wasoun, Michael Wilson and Robert Wilson. What became of these men is not known.

Similarly, in 1582 William Gilmour of Polquhairn, in Ochiltree parish, was called before the Lords of Council in Edinburgh on a charge of witchcraft and sorcery. He was sent to appear before the justiciar of Ayr but there is no further reference to him known.

In 1586 or 1587 the witch of Barnweill, a former parish now incorporated within that of Craigie, was burned in Ayr. Who the witch was is unknown, but she must have been tried locally and found guilty of sorcery and other crimes. That she existed and was killed is confirmed from the expenses for this execution being recorded in the burgh accounts - £7 3s 8d Scots for candles, meat and drink, pitch barrels, coals, 'roset, hedir, treis and uthir necessaris.'

In 1595 Marion Grief was burned as a witch in Ayr, her execution requiring coals, cords, tar barrels 'and other graith' costing £4 4s in total. Slightly luckier was Margaret Reid, who was found guilty of witchcraft in 1596. According to the minutes of Ayr Presbytery she was banished to remain outside the burgh.

A number of notables have been noted for practising witchcraft over the centuries. John Boswell, the laird of Auchinleck in the sixteenth century, was a notable example. On 5 March 1591 he was ordered to appear before the Privy Council. It was noted that 'not onlie hes oft divers tymes consultit with witchis, bot alsua be himselff practized witchecraft, sorcerie, inchantment and uthiris divilishe paractizeis, to the dishonnor of God, sklender of his worde, and grite contempt of his Hienes, his authoritie and lawis.' John Boswell failed to appear before the Privy Council and was denounced a rebel. On 28 February 1592 Richard, or Ritchie, Grahame was burned at the stake at the Cross of Edinburgh for his associations with witchcraft. In his final confession, he told the crowds that he had raised the devil 'in the Laird of Auchinfleck's dwelling-place'. This probably referred to the Boswell town-house in Edinburgh, rather than the old Castle of Auchinleck. Boswell himself died in 1609.

In 1599 Janet Young was burned in Ayr for being a witch. The Ayr Burgh Accounts record the cost of such an execution; £4 (Scots) to Barquhill the hangman, £1 for a tar barrel, 7s 8d for a rope and coal.

Four cases of witchcraft appear from 1605. In that year Margaret Duncan, Janet Hunter, Patrick Lowrie and Katherine MacTear were tried. This appears to have been Katherine MacTear, or MacTeir's second trial, for she was on record as having been tried in 1602, but she must have got off on that occasion. She was probably a resident of Dundonald parish, and survived her trial. At the trial of 1605 the outcome is not known. Similarly, what happened to Margaret Duncan is not known.

On the night of All Hallows (Halloween) Patrick Lowrie is said to have met with the Devil. The 'Earl of Hell' supposedly gave him a belt made from hair, the end of which had a metal buckle shaped like a claw in the form of a hand. Lowrie admitted at the trial that he was in the habit of going to abandoned kirkyards and digging up corpses. These he was able to use in creating his spells. He was also indicted for consulting a local witch, Janet Hunter, who was tried and executed in 1605. The court found Lowrie guilty, and he too was to suffer execution.

A witch named Bessie, or Elizabeth, Bell was executed in Ayr in 1613. Little is known about her other than she suffered death, having been found guilty of witchcraft.

Archibald Dean, a burgess of Irvine, was married to Margaret Barclay. Margaret was accused of being a witch in 1618, following her supposed cursing of a ship on which her brother-in-law, John Dean was sailing. John Dean had stolen from Margaret, and her sister-in-law, Janet Lyal, had slandered her. Margaret had brought these accusations before the Kirk Session, which recommended reconciliation. They were told to shake hands and make up, in front of public witnesses, and this they did, but it was not enough to quell the problem.

Margaret was unhappy at this verdict, and though she did agree to forgive her relatives, the problem still annoyed her. When John Dean, skipper of a boat named *The Gift of God*, which belonged to Provost Andrew Train of Irvine, was setting out from the harbour, Margaret was heard to have cursed the ship, hoping that it sank to the bottom of the ocean. It so happened that the ship failed to return to port at the due time, and the residents of the town began to remember Margaret's curse. The provost sent for one John Stewart, a beggar and clairvoyant, who told him that the ship had been lost at sea, with the drowning of all its sailors. It was later discovered that Stewart had in fact been correct, for the boat sank off Padstow in Cornwall.

John Stewart was arrested, for his ability in seeing the shipwreck was regarded as being unnatural. Margaret Barclay was also apprehended, for it was well known that she had cursed the boat. At the trial, Stewart claimed that Margaret had taught him the magic skills that he now had. He claimed she and two other women had made clay figures of the provost and his ship, and that the Devil had appeared to them in the form of a black lap-dog. The figures were thrown into the sea, where the water boiled like a cauldron, and turned a deep red blood colour. Barclay was also found to have a piece of rowan stick, wrapped in coloured thread, on her possession. Despite this being normally used as a charm to fend off witches, and she claimed it was to keep witches away from her cattle, and thus prevent any loss of milk, it was used as evidence against her. One of the other women mentioned by Stewart was Ishbel Insh, and she too was apprehended.

Insh's eight-year-old daughter was questioned in court, and the evidence she gave was enough to cause Ishbel to be locked up in the belfry of the church. The child may have had flights of imagination, for she told the trial that the Devil had appeared in the house in the guise of a black dog, and that it breathed fire from its mouth and nostrils. Ishbel feared the worst; she expected to be tied to the stake and burnt, so she made an attempt at escaping. She was partially successful in this, but she fell from the tower and was injured, dying a few days later.

John Stewart told the trial that they had gone to the shore and threw in clay images of the boat and its passengers. Margaret Barclay had wished that the sea 'might never bear the ship' and that crabs, or partans as she called them, might eat the crew when they had sunk 'to the bottom of the sea.' Stewart also managed to escape his prison chains and rather than suffer torture, hung himself using ribbons taken from his bonnet.

Margaret Barclay was tortured ('gently', according to the Earl of Eglinton). She was locked up in the stocks, and heavy bars of iron were placed across her legs, squashing them. The weight of the steel bars caused her to scream out in pain, and eventually she agreed to confess. In her confession she implicated one Isobel Crawford. She too was subject to Lord Eglinton's gentle torture, which she suffered 'admirably, without any kind of din or exclamation, suffer[ed] about thirty stone of iron to be laid on her legs, never shrinking thereat in any sort, but remaining, as it were, steady.' Margaret Barclay was later to deny her sorcery, claiming, 'All I have confessed was in agony of torture, and before God, all I have spoken of is false and untrue.' Unfortunately for her and Isobel Crawford, the authorities decided that they were to be tied to the stake and burned to death. Isobel Crawford protested her innocence to the last.

The story of Margaret Barclay was so extraordinary that it attracted the attention of Sir Walter Scott, and he commented on it within his book, *Letters on Demonology and Witchcraft.*

In 1618 Janet MacAllister was executed in Ayr for being a witch. Little else about her is known. In the same year two other witches were tried in the county, probably in Ayr. These were William Nicoll and Malie Wilson. Their case was heard by a local commission authorised by the Privy Council, but what happened to them is not confirmed.

Two cases of witch trials are noted in Ayrshire in 1622. These were of Janet Scott and Maig, perhaps a version of Margaret, Knox of Largs. Some accounts also name the latter as Maig Knock. In both cases a commission was set up to try the women, but the outcome of the cases is not known.

In 1623 an Ayr man named Michael, a spaemen, or teller of fortunes, was sentenced to a period of excommunication.

In 1629 Margaret Wallace was executed in Ayr for being a witch. This is thought to be the same person as Maggie Osborne who is celebrated in the folklore of the town for her evil deeds. A simple cross in the former churchyard surrounding St John's Tower claimed that 'hereabouts is the grave of Maggie Osborne'. The 1855 Ordnance Survey map of Ayr town centre claims that she was 'burned for witchcraft about the end of the 16th century' at the Malt Cross in Ayr, which was located at the junction of High Street with Sandgate.

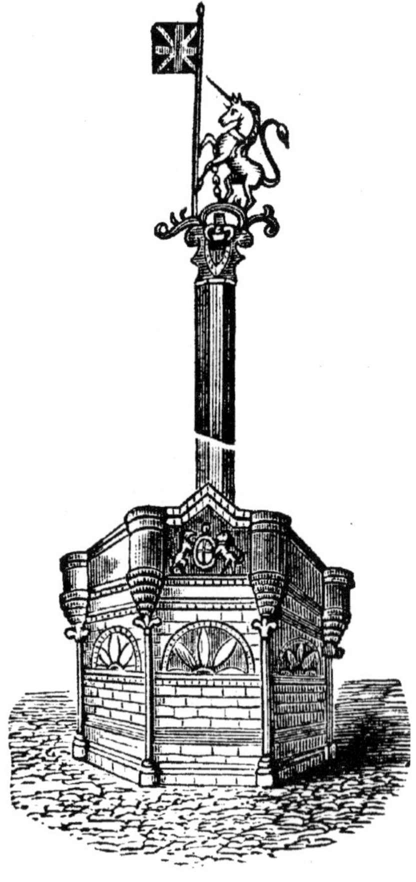

9.2 The Malt Cross in Ayr was where the town's witches were executed. The cross no longer exists. *(Author's Collection)*

It is claimed that Maggie Osborne lived with her parents in an old building in the High Street, opposite what had been the banking premises of Macadam & Co. The site is currently occupied by Marks & Spencer's premises. Maggie's parents died, and she found herself to be the heiress of the building. Although a young and beautiful girl, Maggie seems to have had a mental disablement which frightened people away. Old accounts claim this was a 'brain fever' and that the local minister, Rev William Adair, pronounced that she must have some association with the devil. He tried to get her to confess some connection, but the lass refused. As time passed she became ever more adamant that she had nothing to confess, and eventually she was taken from her home and locked up. As time passed, Maggie seems to have improved in jail, although she was suffering from lack of food and water. At length she stated that 'death would be preferable to a life of confinement', which was translated by Adair into a confession of guilt. Accordingly she was hanged at the cross, before her corpse was removed to St John's churchyard for burial.

The tale has many doubts, however, for there is no reference to a Margaret Osborne in any old burgh accounts, or kirk records, as a witch. A number of Margaret Osborne's have lived in Ayr over the years, and one of them may have been Margaret Wallace to her maiden name. It is known that Margaret Wallace was burned as a witch in Ayr in 1629, for it is recorded in the Kirk Session Records of 12 October that year.

9.3 The site of Ayr's Malt Cross is still marked on the ground in New Bridge Street, in front of a pub known as The Malt Cross. *(Dane Love)*

Maggie Osborne is also associated with some of the more fanciful accounts of witchcraft in Ayrshire. At the head of the Water of Minnoch, south-east of Barr, can be found Maggie Osborne's Bridge. This bridge gets its name from the time Maggie supposedly turned into a beetle. A second bridge, on the Nick of the Balloch road, which links Balloch with Rowantree Toll, is known as the Witches Bridge.

Other witches were tried around the same time as Margaret Wallace. Helen MacPherson, Margaret Kennedy, Janet Thomson and Agnes Campbell were all tried in Ayr on accusations of witchcraft in 1629. What became of them has not been recorded.

At least three witches were tried in Ayrshire in 1630. These included Janet Reid of Ayr, Marion Ritchie of Newton upon Ayr, and Janet Wallace of Ochiltree. Again, the outcome of their trial is not known. Hew Dunbar of Craigie was tried for witchcraft at some time, but when this was, and what happened to him, is not recorded.

In 1643 the Presbytery of Ayr received numerous complaints from the residents of Ayr against one Susanna Shang, who they regarded as having practised witchcraft. They sent to the Lords of Council in Edinburgh to ask for permission to try her as a witch.

In the north of the county, three witches were tried in 1649. Agnes Fleck lived at Hunterston, in West Kilbride parish. Elizabeth, or Bessie Graham, lived in Kilwinning, and Christian Thomson lived at Linn, near to Dalry. Two of these cases resulted in unknown outcomes, but that of Bessie Graham is well documented.

Bessie was arrested for being drunk and disorderly, and for slandering another woman, the wife of John Rankin. Apparently, soon after the rumpus had taken place, Rankin's wife took ill and died. All eyes then turned on Bessie, who was accused of causing her death. She was arrested at the end of August 1649 and locked up in the abbey tower, then acting as a gaol, where she was held for thirteen weeks. During that time she was visited by the local minister, Rev John Fergusson, who found her to be calm and composed, and so 'normal' that he expressed his opinion that she was unlikely to be a witch. He hoped that she would be able to escape from prison.

However, during her time in gaol, Bessie Graham was visited by a witch-finder, or pricker, Alexander Bogs. According to an old account, he found the mark of a witch on 'her ridge-back, wherein he thrust a great Brass Pin, of which she was not sensible; neither did any blood follow, when the Pin was drawn out.'

With this evidence, the provost sent to Edinburgh for a Privy Council Commission so that she could be tried. In the meantime, Rev Fergusson was becoming even more convinced of Bessie's innocence.

He wrote:

> This put me to manie thoughts and Prayers, wherein I did engadge myself to God, that if he should find out a way for giving me, and the Assize full clearness, either by her own Confession or otherwise, I should remarke it as a singular Favour and special Mercy. This resolution I did often reiterate, Lord make me mindful of it. After a short time, Providence brought to light the unexpected Presumption of her guiltiness, which did convince me more, than any of the rest.

Accordingly, the minister, a kirk officer, and one of his servants returned to the tower to visit Graham. He asked her to make one final confession, but she steadfastly refused to do this. As the minister was leaving, he paused at the tower steps. He heard Bessie say one sentence, but immediately afterwards heard another voice speaking in the darkness. Listening intently, he came to the conclusion that it must have been the Devil. Rev Fergusson remained for a few moments, and again heard Bessie speak. The voice answered again, one that the minister described as being 'low and ghoustie', and he was sure that it was not her voice. It was also heard by the servant, Alexander Simpson.

The minister and others then took Bessie Graham to the school, where she was kept under the guard of six men. On 13 November the minister told the authorities that Bessie was ready to confess, but when this was taking place she spoke in a very quiet voice. The minister asked her to speak up, but she said that she couldn't, else the Devil would give her strength. During the trial she appears to have stared into mid air to either side of her, and this was taken that she was looking at the Devil, whom the rest of the jury could not see.

The trial continued the following day, but Bessie refused to repent, but did admit to being a wicked woman. She hoped that she would be forgiven in heaven. As the trial continued, she fell to her knees and prayed for forgiveness, admitting that she had lived an evil life and now wanted to die. She was found guilty and was burnt at the stake. She admitted all her crimes, but denied furiously that she had been a witch right up to she breathed her last.

Janet Smellie was a noted witch in Ayr. The first record we find of her is from the year 1613 when she was charged with making slanderous accusations against her neighbours. As a punishment she was tied to the Fish Cross and a gag or 'spurr' was placed round her head, to prevent her from speaking. In 1621 she again appears at the penitents' pillar for her gossip, and as a result attempted suicide by poison. In 1628 she was apprehended and held prisoner in the 'Black House' for women (the gaol) which was located below the tolbooth stair. She was to be fed on bread and water alone, and refused any stronger drink. In 1629 she was charged with witchcraft, but at the time seems to have escaped execution and was banished to stay outwith the county. However, she returned to her home town, for in 1650 she was imprisoned again, and died whilst held in the tolbooth. The magistrates of the burgh, at the advice of the Rev. William Adair, had her body dragged through the streets on a sledge to the gallows where she was burned to ashes.

The kirk session in Ayr noted in their records for 11 June 1650:

> The qlk day the Session considering it to be incumbent to them to concur and give ther help in overseing and exhorting and taking paines upon these yt are or shall be here after incarcerated for the sinn of witchcraft dos yrfor ordeine the persones following being of their number such, and elders and deacons shall for the space twentie four hours per vices both in ye day and in ye night, shall oversie the said prisoners to exhort them to confessione and to pray with them to God, and to take all pains for the furtherance of so good a work.

In Saltcoats in 1650 two women were apprehended on a charge of witchcraft and made appear before the Presbytery of Irvine. Margaret Cooper and Catherine Montgomerie confessed that they had renounced their baptisms, had accepted a new name given them by the Devil, and even had 'carnal copulation' with him. They were also accused of 'sundrie malefices, and drawing on of others to the devil's service.'

In 1650 the Presbytery of Irvine found that:

> ...the sin of witchcraft was growing daillie, and that in the several paroches meikle of the hidden works of darkness was discovered and brought to light in the mercie of God, and that severalls were apprehendit and in firnance for that sin, did meet occasionallie this day to heir and receive the confessions of some, of the said sin of witchcraft, that they might recommend the same to the Lords of Privie Counsell for the issuing furth of a commission of assyse to sit upon the said persons, and after hearing, the presbyterie does judge the confessions of the persons following, relevant to be recommendit.

In addition to finding Cooper and Montgomerie guilty, they also found Janet Robison guilty.

In the middle of the seventeenth century the Irvine area seems to have been a hot-bed for witchcraft, and the Presbytery of Irvine had to try around fifty cases within a period of three months. Of these cases, it is reckoned that twelve women were to be executed in March 1650, followed by four others in the following weeks of April. Previously, in May 1648, Irvine Presbytery decided to send one of its ministers, Rev William Castellan, from his charge in Stewarton to Largs, where he was to investigate a few cases that had been reported. However, Castellan seems to have found little, and reported to the Presbytery that the grounds 'were not so clear as was alleged when they began to ripe them up'.

In Ayr it is known that sixteen witches were executed between the months of March and May 1650. Their names have not been recorded, but reference to them is made in Paterson's *History of Ayr*. Similarly, several witches were executed in Dalry in the same year – how many and whom is not recorded. An Elspeth MacEwen of Dalry is a known witch, but from what period it has not been worked out.

The year 1658 appears to have been a time when the hunt for witches in south-west Scotland was at its zenith, there being considerably more cases in that year than in previous years. Scotland-wide, there were nine reports of witches in Scotland the previous year, whereas in 1658 there appears to have been around 100 witches reported or tried by the ecclesiastical authorities. According to

Christina Larner, in *A Source-Book of Scottish Witchcraft*, of these hundred or so witches, Ayr Presbytery appears to account for around fifty-three witch trials.

Why should there be a sudden rise in witchcraft cases in the county? P. G. Maxwell-Stuart claims that it may have been as a result of the Covenanting struggles. At the time south-west Scotland was living in troublesome times, with episcopacy forced upon many unwilling parishes, and most of the friction was previously directed towards authority and the redcoats. In 1658 there may have been a lull in the persecutions, and the godly took an opportunity to remove or deal with long-standing troublemakers in the area. Thus, those who were at the opposite end of the religious spectrum were seen as suspect followers of the Devil.

The Presbytery of Irvine, in 1658, 'having formerly, upon advice from the justices of the peace, recommended to the several ministers to try within their parishes what persons were under such presumptions of witchcraft as might be recommended to the justices of the peace for taking present course with them.' This resulted in an upswing in witch-hunting across Cunninghame, witches suddenly being found in almost every parish. A total of forty-two suspects were reported to the presbytery, of which four were men. They came from the parishes of Ardrossan, Ayr, Craigie, Dunlop, Irvine, Largs, Riccarton, Tarbolton, and West Kilbride. Seven of those notified went missing soon after, no doubt to avoid trial. They had come from Riccarton, Dunlop (four) and two from Largs.

Three women were called before the justices, Isobel Henderson from Irvine, Janet Ross, who formerly lived in Fenwick, and Janet Steel from Kilmaurs. All three were at the time resident in Irvine. Janet Ross's parish minister was willing to testify that she had confessed that she was a witch. Each of the women apparently confessed that they had formed a covenant with the Devil, had denounced their baptism, and were guilty of casting various spells on humans and animals to cure various diseases, or cause the disease in the first place.

A fourth 'witch' in the Irvine cases was a young girl of ten years. Her surname was Wallace, but her forename was unknown. Child witches were very uncommon in Scotland, and Wallace was one of very few that have been noted. According to the report, she 'had before the minister and several others, who are ready to depone the same, confessed that she was present at several meetings with Satan and others, and had consented to be his servant.'

In April 1658 Janet Saers, perhaps Sawyer or Sawyers, was strangled by a rope hanging from the gibbet followed by her lifeless corpse being burned to ashes in Ayr for her connection with witchcraft. As the noose tightened round her neck, she protested loudly to the crowds that she was innocent. A contemporary account of her execution has survived, having been written by Colonel Sawrey, deputy-governor of the citadel in Ayr, and makes interesting reading:

> Upon Friday 23rd instant, was one Janet Saers, late an inhabitant of this town, according to a sentence passed by the judges, (the assize having found her guilty of witchcraft), strangled at a stake and, after that, her whole body burned to ashes. She did constantly deny that she knew anything of witchcraft, and at her death made a very large confession of her wicked life, and had good exhortations to the living, but remained to affirm that she knew nothing of witchcraft. And, as I was informed by those that heard her, when the minister was urging her to confess, she had these words. 'Sir I am shortly to appear before the Judge of all the earth, and a lie may well damn my soul to Hell. I am clear of witchcraft for which I am presently to suffer'. And so with a seeming willingness submitted herself to death. The people in this country are more set against witchcraft than any other wickedness, and if once a person have that name and come upon an assize, it's hard to get off with less than this poor creature.

Other witches executed in Ayr include Elspeth Cunningham and Janet Sloan. They were tried around the same time as Janet Saers but were not executed later. Elspeth Cunningham was accused of causing the death of various people. She was in a no-win situation, for some accused her of failing to assist those that were ill, whereas if she did assist, she could be accused of using her charms. Mary MacGreen was sick, and her husband sent for her to help. She apparently turned the back of her hand to him, a sign of refusal. When Mrs MacGreen subsequently died, Cunningham was accused of causing the death. Other claims made against her were that she went to the kirk in Irvine and there conversed with the Devil. Another witch, Barbara Melling, came to her defence, stating that when they arrived at the church the door was locked and they could not enter. Theophilus Rankin witnessed the pricker, Thomas Garvane, insert a pin in what was described as the Devil's mark on her body, and it was pushed almost to the head, Cunningham feeling no pain. Others witnessed the pricker on other occasions, William Blair seeing six pins being inserted into her body, and John Rodger seeing a pin being sunk into her body as far as the head, as easily as into butter, with no signs of blood. The jury acquitted Cunningham on a number of points, but there was still enough evidence for her to be found guilty of witchcraft and she was executed on 2 April 1659.

In Ayr a witch named Barbara Cunningham had been accused of quarrelling with one Henry Wallace. He had taken ill, and had blamed his condition on Barbara. When he died soon after, all eyes turned on Barbara, who was accused of causing his death, and having prophesised that he would die a beggar. Wallace's widow, Grissell Black, was also to take ill, and Barbara asked her servant how she was keeping. The servant replied that she had been through some rough times, but was getting better. Barbara apparently replied, 'It was little that she had suffered in respect of that she would suffer,' which was taken as evidence that she was predicting troubles ahead. Other accusations made against her included the story that she caused a house fire when she had been annoyed by its occupants, and that when a local Baillie, John Love, who had previously fined her two dollars, asked for assistance with an illness, she refused to help. Many claims of what she had said to others were being taken as evidence of her association with the devil, though many of these were no more than 'rough-talk' for a woman: 'Aye, the fellow's horse is dead, but my malt is still in the mill', or 'Blow wind in its arse.' Barbara did not get on with her son, and they often publicly quarrelled. When he died before her, she was accused of killing him, too. The jury in the case could not find her guilty of witchcraft, but did fine her £30 as a caution for her good behaviour.

The many witches tried in 1658 included the following: Margaret

Allan, Janet Boyd, Janet Flowan, Bessie Fullarton, Janet Gillespie, John Gillilaw, Annabel Gottray, Janet Graham, Janet Hamilton, Janet Holmes, Christian Hunter, Margaret Jameson, Margaret Lorimer, Marion Leiges, John MacKie (Craigie), Janet MacSkimming, Christian Meving, Marion Milliken (Craigie), Catherine Mogersland, Agnes Mortoune, Janet Murdoch (Craigie), Agnes Paterson, Margaret Patoune, Janet Reid, Agnes Robson (Craigie), Janet Salber (who is known to have been executed), Margaret Sunderland, Janet Symson (Craigie), Marion Symson (Craigie), Janet Tait (Craigie), Heline Thom, John Walker, Agnes Wallace, Agnes Wasoune (Craigie), Janet Wilson and Bessie Woodside.

In 1659 John Laurie of Craigie was tried on a charge of witchcraft, but his punishment is not known. In Mauchline in 1671 Marion MacCall was tried for witchcraft. She was found guilty of some degree of the craft, but not enough to have her executed. She was punished by other means.

In Largs five witches were tried in 1662. These were Agnes Clerk, Janet Crawford, Jean Dunbar, Marjory Scott and Christian Small. They were tried by a local commission sanctioned by the Privy Council.

A Kilmarnock woman was executed for witchcraft in 1673. Janet MacNicol had lived in the town for many years, but for some reason moved home to live at Rothesay on the Island of Bute. It was there that she first came to the notice of the authorities, and some of her practises were suspect. Whilst she lived in Kilmarnock her behaviour does not seem to have caused any untoward concern, but on her arrival on Bute she seems to have caused a stir amongst the locals. They claimed that she had been guilty of practising the 'vile and abominable crime of witchcraft' in Kilmarnock for twelve years. The Bute folk decided that she was guilty of the crime, and consequently she was taken from her prison cell out to the point known as the Gallows Craig at Rothesay. There, where criminals were hanged, Janet MacNicol was strangled to death.

Major General Montgomerie, who lived in Irvine, discovered that some of his silver plate was missing in February 1682. He immediately suspected one of the female servants in the house, but she flatly denied any knowledge of this. However, she did offer to help the Major recover his silver, and went about it in the following manner. On the appointed day, she took a Bible down into the laigh cellar of the house. There on the hardened clay floor she drew a large circle, around herself. She then turned a riddle on end twice from north to south, or from the right to left hand. All the while she held in her hand nine feathers, which she had plucked from the tail of a black cock. The servant girl then began to read the 51st psalm, before turning to the book of Revelation. She read Chapter 9, verse 19 backwards – 'Hurt do they them with and heads had and serpents unto like were tails their for tails their in and mouth their in is power their for'. A figure appeared in a seaman's blue cape and asks her what she desired. The servant asked him where the silver was to be found, and he responded with an answer. She then threw three of the cock feathers at the seaman, extolling him to return to whence he had come. As she did this he gradually disappeared. A similar performance was carried out a further two times, when the devil appeared to her, revealing the location of the Major's silverware, and on further search the missing items were accordingly found. Despite receiving the servant's help in locating his stolen goods, the Major reported her to the authorities and she was locked up in the gaol. She subsequently confessed to being a witch, revealing that she had learned her art of white magic from a Dr Colvin, who used to perform it in Ireland.

Margaret Dougall of Ayr was tried on suspect of being a witch in 1682. In the following year there appears to have been a serious outbreak of sorcery in the town, or else a particularly keen witch-finder, for there were nine people tried that year on charges of witchcraft. These were Thomas Boyndie, Janet Fisher, Joan Graham, a female surnamed Hopkin, Catherine Lorimer, Janet Losk, Marion MacRae, Isabel Reid and Helen Wilson. The case against the witches and one warlock was unsuccessful and they were all acquitted.

Probably the last witch to be tried in Ayrshire was one Marion Brown, who is noted in Kilmarnock in 1709.

A legendary witch associated with Ayrshire was Geils Buchanan. Apparently she lived in 1588, at the time of the Spanish armada, for she is credited with sinking one of the Spanish vessels off Portencross. The sinking of this ship is true enough, for in 1740, by using early diving machinery, a man was able to sink below the surface of the firth off Portencross Point and see the remains of the boat. This early experiment in underwater excavation was recorded by none other than Daniel Defoe, noted as the author of Robinson Crusoe. The divers were able to obtain a number of brass and iron guns from the vessel, all of which were dispersed. One cannon, however, made from brass, was long kept on the headland at Portencross. In recent years it was removed to the visitor centre at Hunterston Power Station. Geils Buchanan, however, cannot be verified, but an old local tradition claims that she cast one of her spells, resulting in the vessel going down. She was supposed to have made her way to the furthest point of the castle headland and there taken out a spindle and a length of thread. As she twisted and turned this, the vessel was overcome by the waves and sank beneath the waves of the firth.

9.4 Ardrossan Castle, the ruins of which was said to be the home of the wizard, Michael Scott. *(Author's Collection)*

Another legendry warlock was Michael Scott, who is supposed to have lived in the ruins of Ardrossan Castle. Local tradition ascribes him to being the son of a mermaid, who had an encounter with a sailor. He is supposed to have been quite a good warlock, in so far as he did good for the locals. One of the tales associated with him claims that he met the devil and began to banter with him. Eventually Scott challenged the devil to carry out a task for him, to prove just how clever he was. The devil agreed. Michael Scott requested that he should build a bridge from the mainland of Ayrshire at Hunterston across the Fairlie Roads to the

Island of Great Cumbrae. The devil thought this easy, and set about the task with gusto. He gathered together many stones from the sea and began piling them together across the two mile gap. As he was busily working he was approached by a man who was unaware of who the builder was. He studied the engineering job with great amazement, but when he expressed his admiration to the devil, who had hitherto unnoticed him, the de'il disappeared in a blinding eruption of flame. As he did so, the bridge that was almost complete tottered and fell into the sea. The tale was used to explain why on the island there was a spot where the underlying sandstone was covered with a dark vein of whinstone, known to this day as the De'il's Dyke, and why at the Brigurd Point near Hunterston there are large areas of the foreshore covered with boulders, seemingly arranged in fairly regular lines. The latter has also been ascribed to being the remains of a Roman harbour or pier.

This Michael Scott is also supposed to have saved Scotland from an early form of taxation, known as 'Pow Sillar'. This was properly known as 'poll cess', and the inhabitants struggled to afford it. Michael Scott reckoned that it was unfair, and decided to travel across Europe to Rome, where he would appeal to the Pope. This he did on his famous horse, which supposedly could fly. Climbing to the top of Ardrossan Castle tower, he mounted the horse, told it to 'Munt and flee', and soon arrived in Rome. On getting an audience with the Pope he warned that his horse would neigh three times if his request was refused. At first it was, whereupon his horse gave a great 'nicher', as the old account has it, sending tremblings through the streets of Rome. A second 'nicher' followed, which made the clay chimney pots of the city fall from the roofs, crashing onto the streets. Before the horse could neigh for a third time, the Pope had acceded to his request, and the 'pow sillar' tax was cancelled.

A warlock is said to have lived in the Dunlop area many years ago. He went by the name of Tam Giffen, and tradition claims that in the late eighteenth and early nineteenth century he was a frequent visitor to the parish. Writing in 1852, James Paterson noted that there were many anecdotes about him 'of a marvellous kind, which appear to have been believed by the peasantry until within a later period.' The locals reckoned that he would leave his home in the middle of the night and meet other evil beings, such as ghosts and fairies, and plan their mischief. One morning, when a local asked where he had been the previous night, he replied, 'I was just at a meeting o' witches, an' we settled it yestreen, that the wee wean at the Grange is to dee the nicht.' Naturally, the tale of the child's death was to come about, much to the amazement and wonder of the believers.

An old sailors' tale from Largs recounts the story of a witch from Inverkip who gave shelter to a sailor lad named Jack from Largs one night. As the boy sat in the corner of her hut a second witch entered and went to the cauldron in which some sort of brew was being made. The witch drew out a nightcap from the cauldron and placed it over her head. 'Hilloa for Kintyre!' she shouted, and promptly disappeared, the cap falling to the floor. The first witch lifted it and she also placed it on her head, shouting the same words – 'Hilloa for Kintyre!' When the cap fell to the floor the sailor lad felt bold enough to lift it up. He placed it over his head and shouted 'Hilloa for Kintyre,' like the witches. Within seconds he found himself flying across Arran and the Kilbrannan Sound and landed at a remote spot where a gathering of witches and warlocks were listening to a lecture by the Devil. At one point the devil suggested they should all spend the night in the wine cellar of the King of France, and soon they found themselves in the cellars, sampling the finest of wines. Jack the sailor joined in, but unfortunately he became rather inebriated from the wine. When he swore an oath, no doubt mentioning God or some Biblical reference, the witches all stopped and looked at him. Within seconds they disappeared.

The following morning Jack the sailor was discovered in the king's wine cellars, surrounded by dozens if not hundreds of empty bottles. The king was incensed, and the order was given that he should be hanged that very day. Just as he was being dragged from the cellars by the armed guard, he begged that he be allowed to wear the cap that was lying on the floor. As soon as it touched his head in desperation he yelled out, 'Hilloa for Largs!' The guards were left with no prisoner, and Jack the sailor flew through the air, landing at the Bowen Craigs, south of Largs. Once he had landed he walked back to his home in Largs. Though he lived happily for many years thereafter, he never meddled with the underworld again.

It is said that by the side of the old Routenburn Road, north of Largs, the site of the Witches' Hut could still be seen for many years, located close to Routenburn farm.

The church often rebuked parishioners for taking part in activities that it regarded as being associated with witches or the devil. When in 1735 a man and his wife in Ardrossan parish had been robbed, they consulted a fortune teller in Paisley. However, the church saw this as little less than consorting with evil spirits and sentenced them to excommunication. Similarly, in Galston in 1724 John Craig in Midlands farm had some property stolen from him. He appears to have gone to Glasgow, where he consulted with a woman, known as a wizard, to see if she could assist in its return. The minister found out about this, and spoke to him about his sinful actions, which Craig could not see was wrong. The minister rebuked him, and in the pulpit the following Sunday warned the congregation against such wicked practices.

Witchcraft trials ended in 1736, when the witchcraft laws were repealed in Scotland.

CHAPTER TEN

CURSES

I have already recounted the story of the mermaid at Knockdolian Castle that placed a curse on the family in the 'big hoose' for destroying its home. A number of other Ayrshire castles and mansions have had similar curses placed on them, at least in tradition, and this chapter will recount some of these.

An ancient legend claims that Sorn Castle, which stands on a sandstone cliff above a sharp bend of the River Ayr, will be destroyed at some point in the future when one half goes on fire and the other half falls over the cliff into the river. Why the curse was placed on the castle is no longer known, but the tradition of it appears to have been taken quite seriously for some time. Indeed, in 1907-14, when the present balcony on the river side of the castle was being erected, the curse was remembered. The architect was informed that the curse existed, and accordingly he took steps to ensure that whatever he was responsible for building could not be blamed for any collapse into the river. Thus, when the balcony was being built, it was designed in such a way that no masonry of the original castle was disturbed, and the new stonework was not tied into the existing walls. It was stated by the architect that should his work collapse into the river then it and only it would fall, and his designs could not be blamed for pulling any of the remaining castle with it! So far both the original castle and H. E. Clifford's additions have not collapsed, and neither has it suffered from any fires.

During the time when many Ayrshiremen stood against authority and upheld the National Covenant, an incident took place in the Cumnock area resulting in a curse being placed on a local farm. The Rev David Houston, an Irish minister of the Gospel, had been

10.1 Tradition states that half of Sorn Castle could fall into the river, and the other half be destroyed in flames. *(Dane Love)*

persuaded to come to Scotland and minister to the Covenanters. He was a colleague of Rev David Renwick, who was to be hanged from the scaffold in the Grassmarket, Edinburgh, on 17 February 1688, the last Covenanter to suffer public execution for their faith. Houston was seen as being the next in line as the head minister to the Covenanters, but he was apprehended in Ireland in January 1688. The authorities sent him back to Scotland and he was held prisoner in Ayr for a short time en route to trial in Edinburgh. The king's dragoons collected him once more and set out for Cumnock, where they spent another overnight at an old inn in the village known as the Blue Tower, around 19 June 1688. Apparently this building was taller than the adjoining buildings and had been painted with a light blue wash.

The locals in Cumnock discovered that Houston was being held in the inn, and being a stronghold of Covenanter supporters, arranged amongst themselves to facilitate his rescue the following morning. At Bello Path, east of Lugar, and two and a half miles from the centre of town, the Covenanters arranged themselves on the heights above the narrow defile where the road and Bello Water have to snake through a pass. As the soldiers passed through the Covenanters fired their guns and battered their drums, trying to suggest to the dragoons that they were a far superior number than was in fact the case. The soldiers took fright, and most of them ran for their own lives, leaving Houston on the back of a horse.

Unfortunately the horse was frightened by the gunshots, and bolted along the roadway. Houston had been placed on the horse's back, his legs tied under the horse's belly to prevent his escape. As the horse bolted he was rumbled about on its back and eventually turned around, hanging upside-down between its legs. His head was knocked off the ground a number of times, and when the horse came to rest and he was able to be freed, he had suffered numerous head injuries.

10.2 The Covenanter John MacGeachan is said to have cursed the neighbouring farm when they refused to help him. *(Dane Love)*

Houston managed to return to Ireland, but suffered from his injuries for the remainder of his life. He died on 8 December 1696 aged 63 and was buried in the kirkyard of

Connor, Northern Ireland.

In the affray at Bello Path one of the Covenanters, John MacGeachan was seriously injured. He was the farmer at Auchingibbert, east of Cumnock, and he was able to limp his way back home. Ere he was able to reach his farm he called at the cottage or smallholding of Stonepark. He knocked at the door and the occupants answered. MacGeachan asked for some food and help, but the residents were too frightened to give him any sustenance or aid, for to assist the Covenanters could result in serious consequences for themselves.

In the Cumnock area there is a long-standing tradition that John MacGeachan, described in Rev Robert Wodrow's *History of the Sufferings of the Church of Scotland* as 'a singularly pious man', placed a curse on the farm of Stonepark. It is said that he told the farmer that his fields would become unproductive, and that the farm would decay. Whether MacGeachan did place a curse on the farm or not is unknown, for many claim that a Godly man would not have done such a thing, or whether some other local uttered the curse for the farmer's inability to help, the farm at Stonepark did suffer thereafter. It was said by the country folk of the parish that from that time onward the cattle of Stonepark never produced much milk. The field around the farm became barren and would not grow any crops, and over time the actual steading was abandoned and fell into ruins. Today only a few large boulders remain to indicate where it once stood.

John MacGeachan's family was able to erect a small turf shelter in the middle of a small field near to Stonepark for him, adjacent to an old well where water could be drawn. They carried food to him under the cover of nightfall, but his injuries were so severe that he died four weeks after the rescue at Bello Path. His friends buried him at the same spot, and a small headstone was raised over his grave in 1728. In 1836 a larger memorial was erected alongside.

Penkill Castle is a rather fine old tower house, perched precariously on a steep headland between two burns, above the tiny clachan of Old Dailly, east of Girvan. The oldest part of the castle is the sixteenth century tower, located nearest the end of the promontory, to which additions and alterations have been made over the centuries. At one time the castle was abandoned as a ruin, but in 1857-60 it was restored by Spencer Boyd, who had inherited the remains in 1826. His

10.3 The curse at Penkill Castle has resulted in at least one death. *(Dane Love)*

grandfather, William Losh, was a wealthy industrialist in the northern part of England and he funded the rebuilding of the tower. A massive drum tower containing the main stairway was erected adjacent to the entrance, too large in scale to sit comfortably with the homeliness of the rest of the castle, and a new banqueting wing was added to the east, all designed by the Glasgow architect, Alexander George Thomson.

Spencer Boyd and his sister, Alice, became friendly with William Bell Scott and his wife, Letitia Norquoy, a friendship that was more than platonic, and which became something of a scandal at the time, though the Victorians seem to have ignored whatever went on behind closed doors. William Bell Scott painted an impressive mural on the walls of the spiral stair, based on *The King's Quair,* a fifteenth century Scots poem. In it he incorporated the family members and friends as castle guards, courtiers and characters, as well as Alice's pet duck, Quasi.

In the drawing room a portrait of Spencer and Alice Boyd hangs over the fireplace. It was painted by William Bell Scott and depicts the Boyds in Victorian garb, standing by the battlements of the round tower, gazing over the Carrick countryside towards the firth. On the frame of the painting is the warning, 'Move not this picture, let it be, for love of those in effigy.'

The inscription on the painting has led to the formation of the Penkill curse. After the death of Alice Boyd in 1897 the castle was left empty for some time, and began to run down once more. The last of the family, Evelyn May Courtney-Boyd, an elderly and frail woman of 84 years, remained in the castle until the early 1970s. She was persuaded by a local milkman, Willie Hume, to allow himself and his family to occupy part of the building, but soon after some of the contents of the castle appeared at auction, against her knowledge, but the portrait remained. However, one day the milkman and an antique dealer were trying to remove the painting. As they made attempts at taking it from the wall, the milkman fell down in front of the portrait, choking. Later that night he died from a heart attack. Locals claimed that the inscription had been a warning that the painting should never be removed from the castle.

In addition to the above story, it is said that the milkman's wife inherited the money from the sale of the castle and its contents to a rich American, Elton Eckstrand, on the death of Evelyn Courtney-Boyd. She used the money to purchase a public house, but this failed, losing most of the ill-gotten inheritance, and the last the locals heard of her she was working as a cleaner in a hospital near Perth. Despite the castle having changed hands once more, the painting with the curse still hangs above the fireplace in the Rossetti Room, where it probably will for evermore.

Not far from Penkill, a mile or so up the Girvan valley from the castle, is the country house of Bargany. This house was for many years owned by the Kennedy family, but in later years passed to the Dalrymple Hamilton family, who still own the estate, although the mansion itself has been sold. The legend may explain why the house changed hands.

One day in 1831 Sir Hew Dalrymple Hamilton, the laird of Bargany, left Bargany House and went to the stable where he mounted his favourite horse. He rode along one of the many long drives that make their way through the policies, through the woodlands and by the side of the River Girvan. As he rode he spotted what appeared to be an old woman in front, walking unsteadily towards him. Incensed that someone should be wandering around his pleasure grounds, he pulled up his horse as he arrived by her side. 'Where are you going?' he demanded of her.

'I'm jist going tae the big hoose tae sell some things tae the lady,' she replied.

The laird responded that he thought the lady would not want to be troubled with her trifles, and that she should leave the estate. Indeed, so annoyed was he with her thinking that she should try to sell her wares at his house, he is said to have chased her down the drive, brandishing his riding crop at her.

It turned out that the old woman was a gypsy who was in the area with her family. She had made a number of little gifts which she was trying to sell in order to raise money to feed her children. After being treated poorly by the laird she turned around and shouted in a broken voice at him.

10.4 Bargany House is said to have had a curse killing off male heirs. *(Author's Collection)*

'The craws will leave Bargany for a hunner years, and during that time nae male heir will be born in Bargany Hoose.'

As it turned out the curse came true, for the family were never blessed with sons, and the estate passed through female hands. It is said that sometime after the hundred years had passed, crows returned to the high trees around Bargany House and started to nest once more. The house had been let to tenants, and it was noted with interest that the wife was able to give birth to a healthy son.

A similar story of a curse being placed on a landed family is associated with Busbie Castle. The name probably does not ring a bell for many Ayrshire folk, for the castle was eventually abandoned and it fell into ruins. After standing forlorn with rent stonework for many years, it was deemed as being too dangerous to preserve, and the council ordered its demolition. Today, the site of the castle is just open ground behind Greenhill Terrace in Knockentiber, west of Kilmarnock.

Busbie was an old tower house of the late sixteenth century, rising foursquare in plan through four main storeys plus attic rooms. The castle was adorned with some large arched windows, indicating that it had been erected at a time when defence was not as important as it once was, and the corner turrets were ornamented with stone string moulds and solid stone conical roofs. The only hints at defensive features were the wide gunloops on the ground floor, perhaps included more for ornament than function. Internally, the castle's great hall was located on the first floor, reached by a turnpike stairway in the corner.

Busbie Castle was erected by the Mowat family. They remained in possession up to the early part of the seventeenth century, after which ownership passed to the Eglinton family, followed by the Ritchies. The traditional tale accounts for the initial change of ownership. Apparently John Mowat of Busbie would not respect the Sabbath and failed to appreciate that it should be a day of rest. They were wont to hold parties and entertain guests regularly on a Sunday, despite the protestations of the local minister. He appears to have had no success with the partying Mowats, and at length called on Rev John Welch, minister of the Auld Kirk of Ayr, to assist with his complaints.

Rev Welsh was something of a noted minister at the time. He was a devout Covenanter, and was much admired by the 'gentlemen and persons of all rank, through the shire of Air', apart from the 'openly wicked and profane'. He wrote a number of letters to the laird of Busbie, very civilly it was noted, but Mowat chose to ignore these. Welsh made his way to Busbie and there met John Mowat. The laird invited him in, but Welsh refused. However, he did inform him that he had come with

10.5 The owner of Busbie Castle suffered from a curse made by an Ayr minister. *(Author's Collection)*

a heavy message from the Lord. He berated him at length about his failure to observe the Sabbath, and lectured him on what sort of experience he could expect in the hereafter, should he fail to change his ways. Mowat listened for a while, but soon lost interest in his visitor. Rev Welsh, realising that he was getting nowhere, turned around and left.

As he did so, he spoke to Mowat, placing the curse on the estate. He told him that 'the Lord would cast him out of his house and lands, and none of his posterity should ever enjoy them.'

John Mowat continued as before, indeed, it was claimed that he became even worse, and his family were known to play games, including football, on Sundays. According to the tale, the Mowats were a well-off family prior to the minister's visitation, and after the curse was placed, things suddenly turned worse. One disaster after another seemed to follow, each costing the family considerable sums of money.

The Mowats lost financially in a number of schemes, and within a few years they were forced into selling Busbie Castle, the Montgomerys of Eglinton acquiring it at this time. On the day when the laird of Mowat handed over the keys of the castle to the new owner, he is supposed to have remarked, 'Now Mr Welsh is a true prophet.'

The Mowats must have seen the error of their ways eventually, for a son of the family, Rev Matthew Mowat, became a minister in Kilmarnock. He often related the tale of Welsh's curse on his family, and that John Mowat would relate it to his family with tears in his eyes.

The Montgomerys remained at Busbie for a number of years, but the castle began to break up. In 1847, James Paterson noted that the tower 'has long been roofless, and is falling into decay.' The thick walls were rather deceiving, for in places they had tunnel corridors within them, considerably weakening them. Large cracks appeared in the stonework, and as early as 1889 when a sketch was made in by David MacGibbon and Thomas Ross, for their *Castellated and Domestic Architecture of Scotland*, the walls were broken. The castle had changed hands again by this time (in 1763) and the new owner, James Ritchie, had abandoned it. His son, Henry Ritchie, proposed building a modern Busbie House instead and laid out plantations in readiness for it. It was not built, however, for he preferred to live at Cloncaird Castle, near to Kirkmichael. The surrounding grounds were built on, creating the mining community of Knockentiber, and the proximity of the houses, as well as the possibility of the tower collapsing, resulted in its demolition in 1952.

A story of the curse on the owner of Craigie Castle is recounted in an old book written by Rev Robert Wodrow. He states that when the minister and the kirk session held considerable sway over the populace, and when the Sabbath was kept as a holy day, the laird of Craigie Castle, Sir Hugh Wallace, who died around 1650, was in the habit of ignoring the Bible and the fact that Sunday should be a day of rest. The laird had arranged for some goods to be brought to the castle, and instructed some of his tenants to take their horses and carts to collect the material. The group collected what they were to take to the castle and, in a small convoy, journeyed back to the tower. There was only one major difficulty – the transportation of the goods was being carried out on a Sunday.

A number of ministers in neighbouring parishes, through which the entourage passed, were incensed at the treatment of the Sabbath, and wrote to the minister of Craigie, a Rev Inglis, to inform him of their displeasure. Rev Inglis made his way to Craigie Castle, where he was allowed an audience with the laird. He scolded him for making his men working on the Lord's Day, and berated him for the fact that a number of neighbouring ministers were also much angered at his lack of reverence. The laird replied that the men had been working that day on his orders, and that he supported them fully in what they had done.

10.6 The owner of Craigie Castle was cursed when he refused to rest on the Sabbath. *(Dane Love)*

Rev Inglis ordered the kirk session to order the men guilty of carting the goods to appear before them, in order that a punishment may be issued. However, despite the summons being issued, the men refused to attend, their laird instructing them to ignore the demand.

With the men failing to attend, the minister decided that he would have to do something to inform them of the error of their ways. At the next Sunday service his sermon made reference to their sins, and at great length he denounced them to rot in hell for evermore. The laird of Craigie was at church that day, and as the sermon went on, interminably berating the laird and his men, his anger grew and grew. At length it erupted, and the laird stood up and withdrew his whinger, or short sword, from his side. In anger, he threw the sword towards the pulpit. The minister was quick enough to duck behind the parapet, and the sword passed over his head. Its point stuck into the wooden sounding board at the back of the pulpit.

The minister gradually rose back up, gathered himself together, and addressed himself direct to the laird of Craigie. 'Sir, you have put ane open affront upon God and his ordinances in what you

have aimed at me, and now I will tell you what God will doe to you. Your great house, in this place, shall be reduced to a heap of stones, and he that offers to repair it shall lose his pains; and your son now, whom you have such great hopes of, shall die a fool!'

The curse of the minister came true in part. The laird's son at that time was serving with the army in England. He had been a noble fighter and man of considerable promise. However, perhaps suffering in a fall, or from some disease, he gradually became mentally ill and was to die from insanity soon thereafter. Similarly, Craigie Castle was requiring some renovation work on it, and some masons and labourers were employed to restore the walls. Whilst they were busy on one of the main walls of the castle collapsed and almost buried all of the workers.

Craigie Castle was abandoned as a home fairly soon after the time of the curse, the family deciding to move to their lesser tower house of Newton Castle, in Ayr. After a few years had passed, they built a new country house on the banks of the River Ayr, which was named Craigie House after the old castle. The old castle was left to fall further into ruins, and its hoary walls have risen above the Ayrshire countryside ever since.

CHAPTER ELEVEN

LEGENDARY BATTLES

There are a number of ancient traditional tales that tell of battles fought centuries ago on the moors and glens of Ayrshire. This chapter will look at and retell the stories of the ancient conflicts, for which there is no real historical proof, but which tradition has claimed have taken place within the county. Thus, these battles predate the known conflicts that took place within Ayrshire, such as the Battle of Loudoun Hill, where Robert the Bruce defeated the English foe on 10 May 1307, or the Covenanter battles at Mauchline Muir in 1648, or Airds Moss in 1680.

One of Great Britain's most legendary figures was King Arthur who, with his knights of the Round Table, lived at Camelot and fought against other chieftains and was one of the greatest early kings that ever existed. References to Arthur in historical fact are difficult to come by, and many of the places associated with him are located in England, in particular at Glastonbury in Somerset or Tintagel in Cornwall. King Arthur is said to have been one of the ancient British kings, and thus would have had more of an Ayrshire connection that is at first assumed, certainly in modern times.

King Arthur is supposed to have some Ayrshire connections, however, and in 1988 it was announced to the world that Greenan Castle, perched on the cliff to the south of Ayr, may have been Arthur's Camelot. The announcement was made by Norma Goodrich, a genealogist with Burke's Peerage. She had been researching the history of Greenan Castle, which had been purchased by a client. Goodrich's caveat was that there was more than one Camelot, and that anywhere that King Arthur sat down with his knights to convene a parliament was determined 'Camelot'.

A local tradition in Dalrymple claimed that there was a battle at Barbieston, just east of the village, in AD 360. The tale is recounted in brief in the account of the parish in the old *Statistical Account*, which was written in 1791 by Rev Ebenezer Walker. He only relates a few pieces of information, some of which may be mixed up fragments of tradition and truth:

11.1 Greenan Castle is thought by some to have been King Arthur's Camelot. *(Author's Collection)*

> A battle is said to have been fought between Dick of Barbiston and Kennedy, the latter of whom was killed. And from the stone which killed him, the place is reported to have been called *Barbarous Stone*, or Barbiston. Some stones of the old vaults [of Barbieston Castle] were found, and bear the dates of 1340 and 1345. A spear, and several large bones, which dissolved when exposed to the air, were also found near this spot.

Some old historians, such as Raphael Holinshed, writing in the late sixteenth century, and Rev John Spottiswoode (1565-1639), writing in the early seventeenth century, claim that the battle was between the allied forces of the Romans and the Picts against the Scots. Apparently Maximus, a Roman prefect, persuaded the Picts to join the greater forces of Rome in a battle against their old enemy, the Scots. The Roman and Pict forces made their way westward into what is now Ayrshire and came upon the Scots, who were camped by the side of the River Doon. The Picts and Romans attacked at nightfall, taking the Scots from the rear, and virtually routed them. Their king, Eugenius, as well as most of his nobility, were slain in the conflict.

In 1804 Mr Fullarton purchased the farm of Barbieston to add to his Skeldon estate. Soon after, he decided that he would create a new drive to Skeldon House and, whilst the foundations for the road were being excavated, the workers unearthed a stone coffin containing bones, on Barbieston Holm. The coffin had been buried within a small hillock composed of gravel, a material that was desirable for bottoming the road. The coffin was opened, and within it was found a skeleton of a man of considerable size. One of the bones, the right thigh bone, was held against Mr Fullarton's leg for comparison, and he found it to be much larger than his own, and he stood five feet eleven inches tall. It was reckoned that the bone belonged to some 'tall, powerful man, some chief or captain.'

Near to the spot where the coffin was found a stone cairn was also noted, and two others were located in the vicinity of the village at St Valley and Priesthill. These were removed in the first half of the nineteenth century, and each was found to contain both human and animal bones, as well as some heads of spears, spikes and other weapons. The cairns were said to have been the burial places of the dead from the battle, the bones being from humans and horses.

In the eastern fringes of Ayrshire, on the boundary with Lanarkshire, is a deep glen through which a stream, called the Glen Water, flows. This stream rises on the moors, now afforested, of Overmuir, and drops quickly through a steep-sided valley to Darvel, where it joins the larger River Irvine. In this glen it is said that a battle was fought sometime around the year AD 542 between the Celtic people of south west Scotland and the Angles and Saxons, who had pushed their control into these territories. King Arthur was the leader of the Silures, brother Celts who had their lands in south Wales.

The Celtic brotherhood came together to fight the Angles, and the two sides were to meet in the Glen Water area. This was to be just one of around one dozen battles that the Celts fought under Arthur against the Angles.

In the Glen valley at Darvel are a number of antiquities that some say are associated with the battle. By the side of the Mucks Water, a tributary of the Glen Water, is the Carnals Castle, a rounded knoll on a high point surrounded by the water on three sides. As well as being a place of defence, this may have been one of the spots where the dead from the battle were interred. Another Carnals name survives in the glen about one mile further upstream. Carnals Craigs is a rocky outcrop overlooking the Glen Water, and again, may be where the dead were buried. On Glaister Law, at the mouth of the Glen and overlooking the upper Irvine valley, are three ancient burial cairns, perhaps dating from the Bronze Age, but also possibly used to bury the corpses from the fight.

Arthur was to be killed by his own kin. Modred, his nephew, an illegitimate son of his sister, slew him at the Battle of Camlann. Arthur was buried at Glastonbury.

An early battle that is said to have occurred in Ayrshire took place at Mauchline. According to the Ulster annals, the Cruithne, which was another name for the Picts in this area, invaded Ayrshire in AD 681. The Cruithne made their way through the county, claiming the lands as their own, until at last they reached Mauchline. At that point they were met by the people of the ancient Strathclyde who lined up in battle. The conflict was bloody, but the Cruithne were defeated. The spot where this battle took placed is not readily known, but it has often been said that it was on Mauchline Muir, in a similar spot to where the Covenanters were to fight almost a millennium later.

Probably Ayrshire's greatest shadowy hero from the past was Old King Cole. At least, that is how we remember him today, from the well-known children's nursery rhyme,

> Old King Cole was a merry old soul,
> And a merry old soul was he,
> He called for his pipe, and he called for his glass,
> And he called for his fiddlers three.

This is a more modern version of a much older ballad, which ran to five verses, though the lines were repetitive. The first verse of the original version ran as follows:

> Old King Coul was a jolly old soul,
> And a jolly old soul was he:
> Old King Coul he had a brown bowl,
> And they brought him in fiddlers three;
> And every fiddler was a very good fiddler,
> And a very good fiddler was he.
> Fidel-didel, fidel-didel, went the fiddlers three:
> And there's no a lass in braid Scotland
> Compared to our sweet Marjory.

The following verses were as the first, but with the replacement of fiddlers with pipers three, who would 'ha-didel, ho-didel', in verse two. In verse three the harpers went 'twingle-twingle, twingle-twangle', in verse four the trumpeters went 'twara-rang, twara-rang' and in the fifth verse drummers joined in, going 'rub-a-dub, rub-a-dub'. In each case the verse became longer, repeating the line of the earlier verse, much as 'Music Man' does today.

The most probable original King Cole to whom this poem refers was King Coel, or Coilus, who was a provincial king who lived in this part of south west Scotland. Some also say that he could have been a Welsh invader. The period in which he lived is the subject of debate –

Hector Boece states that he died as early as 300 years before Christ, some accounts place his death in the third century, others claim he lived around 500 AD, whereas others are more precise and claim that he was killed in 702 AD. At this time southern Scotland was still made up of independent kingdoms, established in the immediate post-Roman period.

Information on this king is sparse, but according to Andrew Wyntoun (*c.* 1355-1422), who compiled an *Orygynale Cronikil of Scotland* around 1400, Cole was the father of one of the most beautiful ladies in the land. In his account, she:

> ... excedyt of bewte
> All the ladys of that cuntre,
> That nane in Brettayne was sa fayre.

King Cole was engaged in a battle between his men and those of Fergus, a chief of the Scots, who occupied the western seaboard of Scotland. The exact location of this battle is not known, and there have been a few places cited as the battlefield. Some say that it took place near to the mouth of the River Doon, on land that is now built upon by the town of Ayr. Other accounts place the battle near to Waterside, between Patna and Dalmellington. The third possible location of the battle was on the level ground at Dalrymple.

That a battle did take place is well documented. Early historians such as Hollingshed, Hector Boece (*c.* 1465-1536) and George Buchanan (1506-82), make reference to the battle. Boece, who was the first Principal of Aberdeen University, noted that 'Kyle is namit frae Coyll, Kyng of the Britons, quhilk was slain in the same region.'

The details of the actual battle are more difficult to piece together. All that we known is that the Picts and Scots decided to unite their armies and desist from fighting between themselves to concentrate on the Britons, who occupied the territory that is now southern Scotland. Previously the Britons had held the upper hand, having the backing of Rome, and the advantage of being more civilised.

It is claimed that the Scots and Picts came in the night to the camp of the Britons under King Cole and attacked them. Buchanan claimed that the united armies put 'almost the whole of them to the sword'. The

Britons had been drinking and feasting in the evening, and went to sleep in their camp. Fergus heard of Cole's condition and decided that the time was ripe to attack. He made his way to the camp, which appears to have been in the vicinity of Loch Fergus, a small loch to the south-east of Ayr, on the border with Coylton parish.

An old poem, written around 1631 by the schoolmaster of Ayr, John Bonar, gives an early account of the traditional battle:

> The Britones marchet, tuo dayes before the feild
> To Marrok's mote, for easement and for beild;
> Afore the night they waughtet liquor fyne,
> Lyke filthie beasts lying like drunken swine.
> Quhen Fergus heare they wer in sutch a pley,
> Doune fra Craigsbian he came right suddenly,
> And tooke his will upon his traitrous foes,
> Quhair thousands lay skatteret like windlestroes.
> Coylus he fledd unto the river Doune,
> Quher drownet were, many yt thair did runn,
> And northward held quhil they cam till a muir,
> And thair wes stayet be Scots that on him fuir.
> Fergus he followet and came right heastilie,
> Quhair Coyll was killet and all his hole armie;
> The cuntry people fra thenseforthe does it call
> Coylsfield in Kyll, as ever more it sall.

King Cole suffered in the battle and was mortally wounded. However, he is thought to have managed to escape, rushing eastwards towards the Water of Coyle, which may have been named in his honour. The watercourse was in spate, and the men had to head upstream to find a spot suitable for crossing. At length, near to the present Knockmurran farm, south of Drongan, Cole and the remnants of his army found a place where it was feasible to cross. King Cole managed to jump onto a large boulder in the middle of the water, from where he leaped to the opposite bank. For centuries this spot was known as the King's Step.

King Cole and his men then headed north. They were able to cross the River Ayr near to Stair and arrived on the northern banks. The Scots under Fergus were still in pursuit, and at a spot near to Failford they caught up with the flagging army under King Cole. In the battle that followed, King Cole was unable to withstand the pressure put on him by Fergus's men. His army was defeated, and he himself was killed.

In the immediate vicinity of Coilsfield Mains farm in the parish of Tarbolton are three ancient place-names that indicate that something of importance in the military field took place here. There is a spot known as the Dead Men's Holm, so called from the fact that it is thought that the many dead from the battle were buried here. Nearby, within a few hundred yards, is a small stream known as the Bloody Burn, named from the claim that at one time it ran red with the blood from the dead soldiers. The stream flows into the Water of Fail on the opposite side of the stream from the Dead Men's Holm.

The Dead Men's Holm is now a valuable piece of agricultural ground. Many years ago, when ploughing was not so intense, the local farmer was able to see the soil being turned over as he walked behind the horse-drawn plough. It is recounted that on this spot he often turned up fragments of bone and small pieces of armour.

At Coilsfield farm are the remains of a large stone cairn that is reckoned to mark Old King Cole's grave. It is believed that he was interred with great dignity on that spot, although the cairn itself probably predates Cole's time – perhaps he was interred in an ancient

11.2 The remains of Old King Coil's grave can still be found near Tarbolton. *(Dane Love)*

Bronze Age burial cairn that already existed there. Huge boulders of basalt form the nucleus of the cairn, and at one time the mound was enclosed by a hedge and planted with oak trees. Today the cairn is much more open and cattle can wander through it.

In the late eighteenth century, when the original *Statistical Account of Scotland* was written, rather than a mound or cairn, the writer comments on a large stone that he thinks was a monument to old King Coil, - 'the rude stone may have been originally placed to cover the body of some chieftain, although not that of him to whom it is ascribed.'

The ancient cairn at Coilsfield was excavated by a group of keen archaeologists in May 1837. Those who carried out the excavation sent a record of what they had found to the parish minister, Rev David Ritchie, who published much of the information in the *New Statistical Account*. In it he writes:

> The centre of the mound was found to be occupied by boulder stones, some of them of considerable size. When the excavators had reached the depth of about four feet they came on a flagstone of circular form, about three feet in diameter. Under the circular stone was first a quantity of dry, yellow-coloured, sandy clay, then a small flagstone laid horizontally, covering the mouth of an urn filled with white-coloured burnt bones. In removing the dry clay by which this urn was surrounded, under flat stones, several small heaps of bones were observed, not contained in urns, but carefully surrounded by the yellow coloured clay mentioned above. The urns in shape resemble flower-pots; they are composed of clay, and have been hardened by fire. The principal urn is 7⅞ inches in height, 7⅞ inches in diameter, ⅝ths of an inch in thickness. It has none of those markings, supposed to have been made by the thumb nail, so often to be observed on sepulchral urns, and it has nothing of ornament except an edging or projecting part about half an inch from the top. No coins, or armour, or implements of any description could be found.

There were other urns found in the mound, but these were

extremely fragile and fell to pieces when touched. These remains were much older than Cole's time, perhaps dating from 1400 to 1000 BC.

In the Coilsfield area a number of ancient artefacts have been unearthed over the centuries. Locals claim that fragments of armour and weapons have been brought up by the plough, though little seems to survive. Similarly, in 1796 a carved stone was discovered near to King Coil's grave, but its present whereabouts is unknown.

Also found in the vicinity of Coilsfield, but when and by whom is not known, was an ancient hunting horn. This must have been discovered sometime before 1630, perhaps around 1615, for reference is made to it in John Bonar's poem. The horn has become associated with King Coil, although it must be admitted that it could have belonged to some other person in his army.

The horn comprises of a bronze flute to which has been added an ornamental band. One end of the horn is small, containing the mouthpiece, around two inches in circumference. The horn is fairly straight to start with, but then curves steeply. It is 25 inches in length, and the open end is around eight inches in circumference, or about four inches in diameter. Tests have been carried out on the composition of the bronze used to make the horn, and it has been discovered that it is 90.26% copper and 9.16% tin.

11.3 Old King Coil's hunting horn is still preserved at Caprington Castle. *(Author's Collection)*

For many years the horn was kept at Coilsfield House, which was owned by the Cuninghame of Caprington family. It is said that the laird used the horn to summon his servants and workmen together for meetings. This is referred to in Daniel Defoe's *Tour through the Whole Island of Great Britain*, published in 1724 but based on a tour of Scotland which he did in 1706 and recorded in his journal. On the Cuninghame's selling the estate in the late seventeenth century to the Montgomeries it was transferred to their other seat of Caprington

Castle, near Kilmarnock, where it still hangs on the wall.

It is claimed that the horn is the oldest musical instrument in existence in Scotland today and recordings of its five notes have been made, available on CD as *The Kilmartin Sessions: the Sounds of Ancient Scotland*. It is also claimed that the horn is the only instance of a bronze horn being found in Scotland, and indeed in Great Britain as a whole they are extremely rare, there being perhaps only one other, located in England. Apparently, they were not uncommon in Ireland.

The earliest appearance of the ballad 'Old King Cole' in print appears to have been in *Herd's Collection*, which was published in 1776. However, it is thought that the song was known long before that, and indeed it has been speculated that the song may even be as old as the time of Robert the Bruce, for the 'sweet Marjory' referred to could be his only daughter, who was married to Walter, Steward of Scotland.

Although there has long been a tradition that Old King Cole was buried at Coilsfield, this was not universally acknowledged, even in Ayrshire. Rev David Shaw, who wrote the account of Coylton parish for the *Statistical Account* in 1790, begins his contribution by referring to the tradition, 'though it is believed very ill founded', that Coilus was killed in a battle in the neighbourhood, and that he was buried in the kirkyard at what became Coylton, the village obtaining its name from the king.

There are others who claim that the Old King Cole in the song had nothing to do with Ayrshire, and that he in fact was a legendary British king who lived sometime in the fourth century. It is said that he was commemorated by the River Colne and the town of Colchester in Essex, although one scholar has disproved this.

A further legendary battle took place in Ayrshire in AD 836. According to tradition, King Alpin, King of the Dalriadic Scots, is said to have attacked the county, which at the time was part of the Strathclyde kingdom. Alpin, who had succeeded his brother as king just two years previously, was keen to make his mark, as well as extend his kingdom. He sailed from Argyll across the Firth of Clyde and landed his men at Ayr. It was a massive force, and the soldiers made their way from the county town up the River Doon towards Dalmellington. Along the way the army laid waste the countryside, robbing and pillaging the homes of those they passed.

The Strathclyde Britons, however, gathered their forces and headed towards Dalmellington to face the intruders in battle. The two sides met at Laight, midway between the present Patna and Dalmellington. There a bloody battle ensued. The Scots were attacked from the uplands around Dunaskin Glen, a narrow rocky defile where the stream cuts its way down from the hill of Benquhat.

In the fighting King Alpin was slain, and it is said that his body was buried in the vicinity, the place being known as Laicht-Alpin ever since, from the old Scots meaning 'grave of Alpin'. It is said that a standing stone marked the grave of the warrior king for at least four centuries afterwards, but that it was eventually pulled down, and Laight Castle erected on the spot.

Alpin's army was routed, and the soldiers made off as fast as they were able, returning to their highland fastness. The dead of the battle, which appears to have mainly been Scots from Argyll, were buried under large mounds, of which one survives on the summit of the Green Hill of Dunaskin, above the village of Waterside.

The Battle of Laicht Alpin, as it became known, was one of the more significant battles to take place in early Scots history. As a result of the defeat of Alpin, his son, Kenneth MacAlpin, was to become the king of the joint kingdoms of the Picts and Scots, his brother, Donald II succeeding.

In 1197, when the town of Ayr was granted its royal charter by King William the Lion, the extent of its control over the local trade was recorded, and it is quite significant that at that time the spot known as Laicht Alpin was included as being one of the limits.

It is not only the place known as Laight at Dalmellington that lays claim to the spot where the battle, and thus the grave of Alpin, was located. At the far south of the county, where the boundary was long disputed, there are two farms bearing the name Laight, Little and Meikle, located just over the boundary in Wigtownshire. This spot has also been claimed as the place where the battle took place, and a number of stones on the moor may mark graves of those slain.

Glen App may get its name from Alpin, as some claim that it means the valley of Alpin, being the place where he was killed.

CHAPTER TWELVE

GHOSTS

Hundreds of tales of hauntings and visions of ghosts have taken place in Ayrshire over many centuries. Some of these appear to be mere stories, whereas others have some form of substance to them, and those who witnessed the apparitions are adamant that they witnessed something that they cannot explain.

An old tale of ghosts took was centred on the parish of Dunlop. A local, named 'Young Robin' by the parishioners, was wont to tell of his meetings with the spirits. It was said that his 'haffets were lyart and gray,' or that his 'locks of hair were hoary and grey.' He had been in Kilmarnock and was returning home towards Dunlop one bright moonlit evening. He was riding on his horse, but he became aware of something, or someone riding along behind him. At first he thought it was somebody else returning from the market, and he expected them to come alongside and perhaps have a blether about the day's sales, and the prices obtained for various goods. The second rider didn't do this, however, so Robin turned around to see who was riding behind. To his surprise he saw that it was a headless man on a horse that also had no head. Taken aback at this, his rode even faster to try to get away. Glimpsing round to see if he was getting away he was frightened to discover that the horseman was still within inches of his own horse's tail. He urged his horse to gallop even faster, and as they rode headlong towards Dunlop, he became aware that the headless horse and the rider made no sound as it galloped behind.

'Young Robin' rode at breakneck speed over the Glazert bridge into Dunlop, but the horse behind was unable to cross the running water, much like Tam o' Shanter's pursuing witches. Instead, the horse and its rider bounded up into the night sky and disappeared in what was described as a 'flaucht o' fire.'

More stories were told by 'Young Robin' about his experiences with the supernatural. On another occasion he was returning to Dunlop from Glasgow with a horse and cart. He was riding along near to Commore, a remote location between Neilston and Dunlop, when he looked from the cart down to the vegetation by the roadside. Suddenly he became aware of a sweet melodic sound, issuing from the bushes. He had heard tales before of the fairies at these bushes, but this was the first time he had experienced anything. Looking more closely he saw hundreds of little green people. His horse seems to have become aware of them also, and it bolted. In the flight the cart was broken, and the barrel on the back, which contained ale, fell from it and shattered on the ground, spilling its contents. It was said that 'Young Robin' would not leave the house after dark from that time onward.

However, the tale was more likely to be invented by Robin as a means of frightening law-abiding people into staying within their homes at night, so that the illegal practice of smuggling could go on unchecked.

At Dalleagles there used to stand a very old house, which had served as an inn for passing travellers. One night a group of Englishmen came to the inn for lodgings, being employed in a local lead mine. For some reason the innkeeper was killed by the miners, and his body was dumped somewhere, never to be found again. For many years thereafter the inn suffered from ghostly sounds that were attributed to the murder. On one occasion a girl servant was sleeping upstairs in the attic of the inn. She was awakened by the sound of what appeared to be a heavy object being dropped down the ladder that lead to the attic. She froze in her bed in terror, too scared to leave it.

Next day the servant lass told the household of what she had experienced, and some of them admitted to having heard the sounds before. Word spread of the ghostly noises, and one local lad offered to spend the night in the loft to hear if the sound returned. With a collie dog for comfort, he climbed the stair to the attic where he lay down on the bed, his dog by his side. He could not sleep very easily, thinking of what he might see or hear, but eventually fell over.

At midnight the dog woke up and began to howl dreadfully. His hair on end, the dog bounded towards his master and jumped into bed with him. Instantly, the strange sound that had been heard before started again. It was like the sound of a body being dragged across the floor, followed by the creaking and banging of a trap door being opened. The sounds stopped with what appeared to be a body being dropped to the floor from the hatch.

Nearby stood an old tower house named Knockshinnoch, the ruin of which has long-since disappeared from the map. A number of folk had gone into the ruins of this tower, only to discover themselves suffering from a feeling of oppression. Great noises and wailings were heard, which seemed to shake the walls of the old castle. One man ran from the tower in terror to the local farmhouse, where he related his experience to the occupants. The farmer and his wife listened in silence, for what he told them was nothing new, for they had experienced the sounds and feelings many times before.

The old country house of Gilmilnscroft, which lies to the south of Sorn, has stood on a site known to have been occupied since at least the sixteenth century. The present house dates in part from the seventeenth century, with wings of the nineteenth century. For many

12.1 Gilmilnscroft House has the ghost of a Covenanter within its walls. *(Dane Love)*

centuries Gilmilnscroft was occupied by the Farquhar family, as it was during the time of the Covenant. It is claimed that the house is haunted by the ghost of one of two brothers. Tradition claims that the laird and his brother supported opposing sides during the time of the Covenanters, and that they often debated the merits of both causes. One evening, fired by alcohol, the argument became so heated that one of the brothers (it is not known which) started a fight resulting in the other being thrown from a window to his death. The surviving brother was thereafter so overcome by guilt that his spirit haunts the house to this day. A number of modern sightings of him have taken place.

Wellwood House no longer exists – the ruins of it are piled loosely by the side of the River Ayr, to the west of Muirkirk. The original house may have been an old Scots tower house, but over the centuries this was extended, lastly in the late nineteenth century, when the house was occupied by James Baird, a local iron and coal-master. Within the older

12.2 The ghost of 'Beenie' was said to haunt Wellwood House. *(Author's Collection)*

part of the house was a stone staircase. On one of the treads was a stain that tradition claims was made by blood spilled when one of the household was murdered. The site of the bloodstain so infuriated the family that for many years servants were ordered to try to have it removed. Armed with scrubbing brushes and bleach, servant girls spent ages trying to get the mark to lift. Often they thought that they had managed, only for the step to dry off and the bloodstain return. It is even claimed that a stonemason was sent for and was asked to take the tread out and replace it with a new one. Once he had completed this task, he mysteriously died within a few hours and the bloodstain returned to the tread. At length the step was covered over with timber treads, hiding the mark. Wellwood House, which historically was a seat of the Campbell family, was occupied by supporters of the Covenanters during the years of struggle, and the bloodstain may have originated at that time. Others claim that the mark was a natural stain in the stone, and that it had been there since the day the stone was laid in the staircase.

In any case, the occupants of Wellwood House always claimed that the house was haunted. The presence of a female spectre by the name of Beenie was felt by a number of residents and guests over the years. It was said that she was a woman who had lived in the house. She was in love with a man, but she was murdered by a third party. Her room was in the original part of Wellwood House, which dated from around 1600, and she is said to have walked from the house to the Lang Plantain, a nearby wood. She has been seen crying and wringing her hands in grief there. Wellwood House was demolished in 1926, since when sightings of Beenie have virtually ceased.

One of the finest ancient castles in the county is Blair, better known as The Blair, or Blair Castle, near Dalry. The oldest part of the castle perhaps dates from the twelfth century, and over the centuries the Blair family have added to it, creating the present ancient stone mansion. Today the house is available as an exclusive let from the family that have owned it for as long as history has known of the place. The castle has its own ghost, a White Lady, who is supposed to have been the wife of one of the early lairds. For some reason the laird decided that she should be locked up in one of towers of the castle and was later imprisoned in a dungeon with her young child and left there to die. Her spirit has been seen, or experienced in various parts of the house to this day.

No-one seems to have seen the female ghost that reputedly haunts Stair House, located by the River Ayr in the parish of the same name. The house is another of Ayrshire's ancient piles, for many years owned

12.3 The appearance of the ghost at Stair House was often preceded by the smell of perfume. *(Dane Love)*

by the Dalrymple family, but in recent years it has passed through a number of hands. The presence of the female spirit has been felt by a number of people, in particular Mrs Lockhart, who tenanted the building for a time. The appearance of the spirit was apparent by the sudden arrival of a strong smell of perfume, one that could disappear as quickly as it came.

Perceton House is one of North Ayrshire Council's offices. The house, which dates from the late 1700s, is located north-east of Irvine, now surrounded by private housing. Workers in the building have experienced strange things, from doors banging closed in rooms that were known to be empty, to the sound of female voices. On one occasion the caretaker was walking around with his Alsatian when it began to bark excitedly. No-one was visible to the caretaker, but the dog could apparently see something in front of him.

In the following chapter the story of Sir John Cathcart, who killed many wives at the Games Loup, south of Lendalfoot, is related. Cathcart was killed himself, and it is claimed that his spirit haunts the ruins of Carleton Castle, the foursquare ruins of which stand above Lendalfoot, on the Carrick shore. Some folk have claimed that in the vicinity of the old tower the sound of Cathcart's screams can be heard, echoing his death.

Ardrossan Castle, the ruins of which stand on the hill that forms the headland of Ardrossan, is one of the most ancient castles in Ayrshire. The ruins are today quite fragmentary, but sufficient of the building survives to indicate that it was at one time an important stronghold. An old story claims that Sir William Wallace was able to kill the English garrison that held the castle in the late thirteenth century. Wallace and his small band found the castle to be virtually impregnable, so he devised a plan. A cottage in the village around the castle was set ablaze, and such a hullabaloo was created that the soldiers from the castle came out to help douse the flames. As they were busy putting out the fire, Wallace's men attacked, capturing them when they were tired from their exertions. The bodies were taken back to the castle and dumped in an old vault, known since as 'Wallace's Larder'. It is not English soldiers that are claimed to haunt the castle, but Wallace himself, his presence having been noted on occasion over the years.

The ruins of Eglinton Castle, a former country house erected 1796-1802 for the Earl of Eglinton, lie to the north of Irvine, within a large country park. The castle became too large for the family to keep up, and it was eventually demolished, leaving only one façade and one corner tower, which is of considerable height. In 1996 two men were walking through the park and came to the castle ruins. They looked up at the tower and spotted the face of a man looking back down at them. Knowing that the tower was closed, and access was not possible, they ignored it. However, within seconds they heard the steel gate rattling and a ghost pursuing them – the most frightening thing that they had ever experienced.

Cassillis House, which lies to the east of Maybole, and which was for centuries the seat of the Kennedy family, Marquises of Ailsa, is said to be haunted by the ghost of Lady Jean Hamilton. It was she who eloped with the gypsies and who had to witness the execution of her lover from the dule tree in the grounds. Some say that her face appears at an upper window, from where she watched the hanging. More on Lady Jean can be found in Chapter 4.

Of more modern ghosts, or spirits or spirits that still make an odd appearance, the county has many. At Cloncaird Castle, which stands above the Water of Girvan, between the attractive villages of Kirkmichael and Straiton, various owners have experienced different forms of paranormal activity. The present castle dates in the main from 1841, but at its rear is the older tower house. A recent owner of the castle, R. H. MacGregor, often spotted a figure on the stair, and he became so familiar with the haunting that it did not bother him. A second strange phenomenon at Cloncaird takes place in the billiard room. When residents are playing billiards or snooker, the balls can suddenly stop or be deflected for no apparent reason. It is almost as though some invisible spirit has leaned over the table and touched the balls. This appears to have happened on numerous occasions, and has become regarded as a recreational hazard.

A number of Ayrshire houses or castles are supposed to be haunted by Green, Grey or White Ladies. Eglinton Castle ruins, which has already been mentioned, is supposed to be the home of both a White and a Grey Lady. Loudoun Castle, which stands in massive ruins north of Galston, and which is now the centrepiece of a theme park, has an ancient central core, around which a massive gothic pile was erected between 1804-11. The castle was destroyed in a major fire in 1941, since when it has been left to rot.

The Grey Lady of Loudoun often made an appearance when the castle was occupied, and appeared at various locations throughout the building. One of the more common places where she would manifest was the factor's office. Indeed, so common did she appear there that the factor often just ignored her. Others have claimed to have seen the ghost of a hunting dog in the grounds. Those who have witnessed this spectre often describe it as having eyes that glow.

A Green Lady is said to haunt Sundrum Castle, which stands above the Water of Coyle, north of Coylton. The oldest part of the castle is known as the Wallace Tower, from it having been erected by a member of that family in the middle of the fourteenth century, but the castle has been extended numerous times over the centuries, and today is subdivided into smaller homes. In the Wallace Tower the old dining room occupies a barrel-vaulted apartment, and it was within this room that the spirit of the Green Lady of Sundrum was at one time a regular manifestation. It has been speculated that she was the ghost of one of the wives of the Hamilton lairds who were owners for many years. Since the castle was restored the ghost seems to have rested, for she has not been witnessed in recent years. Sundrum is one of those grand rambling castles that has a reputation for secret passages within the walls, some of which are said to still exist. In recent years a ghostly monk has been spotted within the grounds of castle, near to the Water of Coyle.

Cessnock Castle stands on a promontory above the Burn Anne, south of Galston. The old keep, which has three storeys plus an attic, dates from the fifteenth century. Mary Queen of Scots came here after the Battle of Langside in 1568, and it is said that one of her ladies in waiting died here. The ghost of the lady has been seen haunting the castle since that time. Some folk claim that the spirit was Mary Queen of Scots herself. Another spirit that has been seen in the tower belongs to John Knox, the great sixteenth century reformer. He is known to have visited the castle in 1556 and some say that they have seen him wandering in the building, quoting scriptures.

12.4 The severed head of Lord Kilmarnock has been seen rolling about the floor of Dean Castle. *(Dane Love)*

Kilmarnock's Dean Castle has a number of ghosts within its ancient walls. Some of these spirits are associated with William Boyd, 4th Earl of Kilmarnock, who was a noted Jacobite and who was executed for his part in the risings of 1745. During his lifetime, servants at the castle kept seeing manifestations of his head rolling about the floor. This was a premonition of Lord Boyd's execution, when he was beheaded. In fact, prior to getting his head chopped off, Lord Boyd told the crowd of the ghostly head at his castle, and requested that four people be allowed to hold a sheet below his body, to catch his head, for he could not bear the thought of it rolling about the scaffold.

Other spirits at Dean Castle include two young children, apparently named Charles and John, who play tricks on the castle staff and visitors. In the castle's Palace Block, the sound of music is often heard, even although no source for this can be found. In 2005 a group of paranormal investigators spent some time in the castle and they were able to make contact with a number of spirits, including a man who is thought to have murdered his wife, Isabella, in 1519. A small pebble also bounced across the banqueting hall on another occasion, recorded by the investigator's equipment, but when no-one was in the room. One of the investigators apparently became possessed by the spirits and started shaking uncontrollably. She had to be removed from the castle for her own safety.

Some ghosts take the form of animals, and a number of hauntings in Ayrshire are of this type. At the southern extremity of the county, the foot of Glen App, the vicinity of Whidana Wood has the reputation of being the haunt of a ghostly black dog. According to the 'Legend of the Black Dog of Finnart', travellers on the road up the side of Loch Ryan often witnessed the sound of the spectral hound after they left the lochside route and turned into the glen, opposite the road into the former Finnarts House. Many of these witnesses had been returning from Stranraer market, so were perhaps the worse of wear from drink, but others who saw the dog bound from the woods were adamant that they were stone cold sober. On one occasion in the 1930s a man and his dog were driving up the glen when he had to brake suddenly to avoid the black dog that had appeared from nowhere. He saw a chain tied around its neck, but it disappeared before the driver could see it more clearly. The man was so shaken that he was unable to drive for some time, and the dog in the car with him whimpered on the seat, every hair on its body seemingly standing to attention.

At Muirkirk, on the eastern fringes of the county, stands a red sandstone building that was erected as an institute for the workers at the ironworks there. Known as Kames institute, the building was latterly used as an outdoor centre and is currently in a much neglected state. Distinguished by its gothic tower with clock, the institute is said to be haunted by a man on horseback. Some guests at the centre witnessed the spectral figure appearing in one of the dormitories. One witness described the spirit wearing a long dark cloak, one that flowed over the horse. Taken aback at the sight, he tried to wake the boy in the bunk above, but the covers fell down, obscuring his view, and when they were removed the ghost had gone.

A number of Ayrshire's old inns have reputations for being haunted. One of these is the Craighead Inn, which stands at the head of Glaisnock Street in Cumnock. The building, comprising random stone rubble, was erected in 1722, following the drawing up of a lease for the property. The rent, stipulated at that time, was £21 per annum plus two hens and two loads of coal. The inn, which was built in the old Scots traditional style of having the gable facing the street, rises to two storeys plus an attic. It is in one of these attic rooms that the ghost was said to appear. Anyone who entered the haunted room was likely to feel weird sensations, and no-one was willing to spend much time there. The regulars in the bar named the spirit 'Marvin', and talk of him was popular for a time. In the 1970s the landlord challenged a number of regulars to raise money for charity by being sponsored to spend the

12.5 The Craighead Inn in Cumnock is reputedly haunted on its upper floors. *(Dane Love)*

night in the room. No doubt fired with spirits of a different sort, the over-night vigil went ahead without any appearance of the spirit, who does not appear to have manifested since.

A second haunted inn was located in Cumnock, but it was demolished in recent years. The Tup Inn was situated in Lugar Street, and whose original landlady was Janet Tear, hence the inn being often called 'Jenny Tear's'. At one time the front of the inn had a flat over it, and in the 1970s the landlord often heard footsteps emanating from it. On investigation, the flat was discovered to be empty, and over the years he came to accept that it was a ghost or something similar that was responsible for the footsteps.

In Mauchline's Loudoun Street is Poosie Nansie's Inn, which dates from 1700. The inn is known today for its associations with Robert Burns, although it was not his favourite hostelry in the village. At the time of Burns, Poosie Nansie's had more of a reputation of being an ale-house and brothel. The poet set his poem 'Jolly Beggars', or 'Love and Liberty' at the inn, where:

> Ae night at e'en a merry core
> O' randie, gangrel bodies,
> In Poosie Nansie's held the splore,
> To drink their orra duddies.

For many years there have been tales of strange goings-on at the inn, though no real ghost sightings. The inn has been the location of poltergeist activity, many objects appearing to move by themselves from one place to another, or glasses flying from the shelves. Dark shadows have been witnessed passing glass doors and the proprietrix, Marion Young, has felt the presence of someone entering her office when she was working there at three o'clock in the morning. Within the inn a child has been heard crying in the corridor to the kitchen, and yet no-one was there.

At midnight on 31 January 2009 a ghost-finding group, known as Spiritfinders Scotland, visited the inn and set up a number of experiments in the building. The machinery was used to sense the existence of spirits, and the conclusion of their time at the inn was that it had many different unseen things within it. The team claimed to have discovered twenty different spirits in the bar, including that of a young girl. They claimed that they did not pick up any sign of Burns himself, but that he may return at some other time.

12.6 A number of spirits are said to haunt Poosie Nansie's Inn in Mauchline. *(Dane Love)*

In Dundonald the Castle View inn has a reputation for being haunted. So regular were the sightings that in 2005 the landlord invited the Dunfermline Paranormal Research Fellowship to the hostelry to find out what was causing the spirits to haunt the inn. The group had previously found that a number of spirits haunted Dundonald Castle itself.

Ghosts are not tied to ancient buildings or sites, for they have also appeared in modern buildings. A former council house in Cumnock's Riverview had a reputation for being haunted for a time. The house, which is located in the estate known as Barshare, was erected in 1960. In the early 1970s the house was occupied by a police constable who committed suicide. Since that time the house was said to be haunted, and no-one would take on the tenancy. A local minister was brought in to exorcize the house, and the service designed to remove restless spirits went ahead. Despite this action, the house continued to be impossible to let. It was eventually sold off, after which no strange goings-on have been experienced.

Ballochmyle Hospital was located in the grounds of Ballochmyle House, east of Mauchline. The hospital was established during the Second World War but continued to operate until 2000, when the new community hospital was opened in Cumnock. At Ballochmyle a Grey Lady was said to appear. She usually manifested in Ward 14, and one of those who witnessed the spirit was Karen Thomson, who worked as a nurse there around 1988. During a spell on the night shift, Karen went for her tea break, but spotted the old lady with long grey hair. At first she wondered who had wandered into the room, but within seconds the old woman faded away.

The former Knockshinnoch mine that existed at New Cumnock was known to be haunted. On one occasion the pit electrician was working underground, repairing electrical panels. As he worked, he felt the presence of someone behind him, and although he was supposed to be working alone, he was not worried, thinking that someone had come to see how he was getting on. At one point the figure advised him what to do, for the electrician had made a mistake. Quickly sorting the error, he turned around to thank the man, only to find that there was no-one there. Now wondering who had been there, he made inquiries, only to discover that no-one had been underground with him at the time, and no-one could explain what he had heard.

Irvine's Cunninghame House, headquarters of North Ayrshire Council, also has a reputation for being haunted. Although only erected in 1976, it stands on the site of a fourteenth century Carmelite friary, and it is this fact that perhaps explains the spirit of a monk that has appeared over the years. A council worker experienced the spirit a number of times in the 1990s, often on the fourth floor, and on one occasion saw it disappear through a wall.

CHAPTER THIRTEEN

OTHER LEGENDS

The old superstitions that our great grandfathers and earlier ancestors believed in have probably now all but died out. Today only simple superstitions like never walking under a ladder or making sure one leaves a visited house by the same door as was entered are still adhered to by some, whereas most folk have abandoned superstition altogether.

In years past superstitious beliefs were much more common, and numerous places had various beliefs associated with them.

Almost every locality has legends claiming that tunnels once existed linking various historic sites, usually castles with churches, or caves with houses used by smugglers. Ayrshire is no exception, and the following can only be a selection of the many spurious tunnels that are claimed to have existed. In most cases, the tale claims that the tunnel has long-since become lost, but despite many examples of excavation there never seem to be any traces of where they once were being confirmed!

One of the tunnels that was supposed to exist linked two Kilmarnock castles, Dean and Craufurdland. These two ancient towers are one and a half miles apart, with the Fenwick Water intervening. Virtually half way between the two castles is a third, Assloss Tower, but this does not seem to get a mention in the legend, despite being a handy halfway point! Legend claims that during the time of the Scottish wars of independence, the troops of Edward I of England attacked Dean Castle but were unable to gain an entry, from the strength of the tower. Not giving up, however, they decided that they would remain camped outside the tower, and starve the occupants into submission. The English soldiers settled down around the castle, and remained there for some time. They made sure that no-one could leave the castle without being killed, and also that no-one from the surrounding area was able to enter. Thinking that they must be on a sure-fire winner, the English soldiers became a bit suspect after three months had passed. They could not understand how the occupants of Dean Castle were able to keep themselves fed and watered over that period, and assumed that they must have had considerable stores within the tower. One day, however, the castle occupants climbed up to the battlements and there held aloft a wide selection of fresh meat. The English soldiers, who had had to rely on hunting locally to feed themselves over the previous three months, were even taunted with the offer of some beef, those held in the tower claiming to have more than they were able to eat. All along, the trapped occupants of the Dean had been able to make their way out of the tower to Craufurdland, and likewise the Craufurds of Craufurdland were able to supply their friends with fresh food.

The old tower of Dean Castle dates from around 1360, and thus is probably not as old as the time of the story. In 1975 it was gifted by Lord Howard de Walden to the council of Kilmarnock and it now forms the centrepiece of a country park. Around the old tower are later additions, including the Palace block of 1460, and the modern, but traditionally-styled, gatehouse of 1935-6. The old tower at Craufurdland probably only dates from 1550, though was no doubt erected on an earlier castle site. Still in private hands, it is claimed that the tunnel was only blocked up in 1810 or thereabouts, when the present Gothic frontage was added to the castle.

Culzean Castle is one of Ayrshire's grandest country houses, basically built to plans by Robert Adam from 1777-85, and extended in 1875-8, but at its core is an ancient tower house, typical of many Scottish castles. Today this tower, which was re-cased by Adam in his castle style, forms the Old Eating Room, Picture Room and bedrooms above. There are a number of traditional tales of various tunnels associated with Culzean. One of the more common, and probably more possible, states that there is a tunnel linking the castle with the caves on the shore immediately below the castle. These caves are ancient, and indeed gave the original name to the castle that was here. Often in the west of Scotland caves are referred to as coves, or even co's, and historically it was Cove or Coif Castle that stood here. The name Culzean was transplanted to this spot by a branch of the Kennedy family who brought it from a property of that name near Kirkoswald.

Today there is no linking tunnel to be found joining the cave with the castle, despite years of stories associating the laird with smuggling brandy and other goods ashore, hiding it in the caves before transferring it up into the castle. As part of investigations made in the cave, a team of archaeologists from television's *Extreme Archaeology* excavated the floor of the cave and explored the innermost reaches of the cavern to find out if the tunnel had been blocked by a rockfall. Despite discovering that household waste had been dumped in the cave for centuries, and that part of the cave had indeed collapsed, there was little to prove, or otherwise disprove, that a link had ever existed.

The caves of Culzean have long had a legend of a ghostly piper within them. The tale has been recounted at numerous spots throughout Scotland, but traditionally goes like this. Wishing to explore the depths of the caves, to find out how far they extended, it was proposed that a piper should enter the cave mouth and make his way through the caverns, all the while playing his pipes. The laird and his family would follow on the ground above, able to follow the piper's route by listening to the drone of the pipes by putting their ears to the ground. Thus the route taken by the cave could be plotted above, and perhaps the termination of the cave discovered. However, the piper continued to play and never appeared back out of the cave. Accordingly, it is claimed that on some still nights the sound of ghostly bagpipes can be heard in the castle, as well as at various points in the estate, in particular on Piper's Brae, a woodland drive in the policies. Some folk claim that the piper of Culzean is only heard when one of the family is about to marry.

The legend of the haunting of the caves at Culzean goes back almost four centuries in records. Sir William Brereton, who travelled along the coast in 1636, paid them a visit along with the son of the laird of Culzean and some servants:

> ...one of [Culzean's] sons, servants and others, took a candle, and conducted us to the cave, where there is either a notable imposture, or most strange and much to be admired footsteps and impressions which are here to be

> seen of men, children, dogs, coneys, and divers other creatures. These here conceived to be Spirits, and if there be no such thing, but an elaborate practice to deceive, they do most impudently betray the truth; for one of this knight's sons and another Galloway gentleman affirmed unto me that all the footsteps have been put out and buried in sand over night, and have been observed to be renewed next morning.

The Dalrymple family originated in the village of that name, located by the banks of the River Doon. An old castle stood at St Valley in the village which was owned by them, but in 1377 the Dalrymples left this place and in 1429 settled at Stair, when William de Dalrymple married Agnes Kennedy, heiress of Stair. The old castle at Stair was superseded by the present Stair House in the late sixteenth century. The Dalrymples of Stair played an important part in the history of Scotland – James, 5th laird, opposed the marriage of Mary Queen of Scots with Darnley and was an important figure in bringing up the infant King James in 1567. John Dalrymple was created Earl of Stair in 1703. It was he who was responsible for signing the papers that authorised the Masssacre of Glencoe, when the Campbells slaughtered a number of MacDonalds in 1692.

13.1 The Dalrymple family arms have connections with the 'Curse of Scotland'. *(Author's Collection)*

The Dalrymple coat of arms comprises of a blue saltire on a gold background. On the saltire are nine gold lozenges, or diamonds. The arrangement of the diamonds on the shield is similar to how the diamonds were formerly represented on the nine of diamonds in old packs of playing cards. The similarity of the layout resulted in the nine of diamonds card becoming known as the 'Curse of Scotland' or 'Scourge of Scotland', an allusion to the Earl of Stair's part in authorising the massacre. The use of the phrase 'Curse of Scotland' is first recorded in the first half of the eighteenth century.

Another old Ayrshire family has a traditional tale behind their grant of arms. The name has been spelled in various derivatives over the centuries, and by different branches, from Cunningham, Cuninghame, and even Conyngham. All branches, however, include what is heraldically termed a shakefork in their arms, which basically looks like a large capital Y. According to some accounts, the Cuninghame family owe their origin to one of the four knights that were responsible for murdering Thomas Becket, Archbishop of Canterbury, in 1170, before fleeing to Scotland. It is claimed that the shakefork, or 'pairle' may derive from an arch-episcopal pall that was used in the murder. However, this story has no foundation in fact, for the Cuninghames are recorded in Scotland long before the murder took place.

13.2 The Cunninghame arms were granted to commemorate how they saved the king. *(Author's Collection)*

The other, more common tale, recounts how Malcolm, son of Freskine, was responsible for saving Prince Malcolm from the pursuing soldiers of Macbeth. The Prince was so close to being caught when Malcolm, son of Freskine, took him to a hay stack and ordered him to lie down. He then took a farmyard fork and threw piles of straw and hay over the prince. The soldiers in pursuit did not find the prince, and Malcolm acted as though he was a farm hand that had seen nothing. The soldiers under Macbeth rode off, and Prince Malcolm's life was saved. He was later to inherit the crown as King Malcolm III, known as Canmore (reigned 1058-93), and he remembered the other Malcolm's part in saving his life, granting him the Thanedom of Cunningham, from which he adopted his surname. For his arms, he adopted a black shakefork which lies on a silver shield. His aid to the prince is also remembered in the family motto, 'Over fork over'.

There is an old tale associated with Kentigern, or Quentigern Hunter, son of the laird of Hunterston in West Kilbride parish. It was the year 1540, and by this time Hunter the Younger had a wife and young family of his own. Hunter was out hawking along the shores of the bay,

13.3 Hunterston Castle has a tale whereby an old woman or witch foretold the death of the laird. *(Dane Love)*

near to Hawking Craig, when he was met by an old woman who had crossed the stretch of sea known as Fairlie Roads on a small boat and landed near to Brigurd Point. It was late in the evening and it was becoming dark. The old woman approached him and she told him that in seven days time he would succeed as the laird of Hunterston, but that he would only remain the laird for seven years.

The death of his father came to pass as predicted, and Hunter lorded it as laird of Hunterston for seven years. However, the prophecy was always at the back of his mind, and he was always aware of when the seven years would be up. As the time approached, a few weeks before the date he was expected to die, he returned to Brigurd Point. In the still of the night he called out to the old woman to come and tell him more. Within a short period of time a laugh is heard across the waters, a laugh that was rather demonic in tone. As he gazed over the Roads to Great Cumbrae he spotted a small vessel coming his way. Soon it landed on the shore and a haggard old woman stepped from it. With long grey hair, unkempt and straggly, the wrinkled woman retold Hunter her tale. Indeed, he would only be laird for seven years, and the time was soon to come to an end.

Within days word of the battles against England reached him, and he felt obliged to join his fellow Scots in the campaign against the auld enemy. After praying with his wife and family, and wishing them farewell, he rode off with some of his men towards Edinburgh. The Scots met the English at the Battle of Pinkie on 10 September 1547, and among the Scots left for dead on the field of battle was the young laird of Hunterston.

A number of gravestones and places of burial have developed legends associated with them over the decades. At Old Dailly, in the Girvan valley, the old kirkyard among its trees seems to have gathered more than it fair share of stories. Such is its romantic location and associations that it seems to appeal to the story teller.

Old Dailly is the resting place of four Covenanting martyrs. Two of these, John Semple and Thomas MacClorgan, are commemorated on an obelisk erected in 1825. The other two martyrs' names are unknown, but one of their graves has been marked for many years. Over it lies a 'rude flat whinstone' which by tradition was the original hearthstone of the martyr's fireplace. The Covenanter lived at a very remote spot called

13.4 Old Dailly is the burial place of some unknown Covenanters. *(Scottish Covenanter Memorials Association Collection)*

Black Clauchrie, which lies far out on the moors five miles east from Barrhill. It is said that the dragoons were in pursuit of him and came upon him at home. Their swords were drawn and one of the strikes made by a blade hit the hearth, knocking a chunk from it. This broken part has been pointed out on the stone ever since. The blood of the martyr was shed on the stone, and it has left an indelible mark on the boulder. When the martyr was secretly buried at Old Dailly, his hearthstone was lifted and placed over his grave. From that day onward the locals would point out the reddish colour on the stone as the shed blood of the martyr. A similar tale to this exists at Stonehouse in Lanarkshire, where the stone erected in memory of the martyr James Thomson, shot at the Battle of Drumclog in 1679, has a hole in it. Should someone put their finger into the hole and retract it, they will find that the martyr's blood has been transferred to it. This has been explained by the fact that the stone contains a red ochre vein, and that the colour is transferred to the finger. At Old Dailly a later memorial was erected to the other martyrs of the parish, and it includes the lines in memory of…

… two Covenanters
one of whom, according to tradition,
was shot dead, while herding his cow
at Killoup;
and the other was struck down on his
own hearth, at Black Clauchrie, Barr,
and is buried near this spot.

There are many stories that have been handed down the generations that try to explain why certain things happened in the past. Some of these may have some basis in fact, whereas others are perhaps just pure fiction, made up and elaborated over the years to entertain the family, at a time when story-telling and recitation was the usual form of family entertainment.

An old tale tells how the estate and castle of Blairquhan passed through three families in quick succession. The castle had been a seat of the MacWhirters for many centuries, and the original foursquare tower that stood there had been known as MacWhirter's tower from its builder. To this, over the centuries, had been added lesser wings, creating an extensive baronial castle. This was demolished in 1820 when the present Tudor Gothic mansion was erected. The last of the MacWhirters died and it was not known who should succeed to the estate. He had no sons, nor direct male heirs. However, he did have two daughters, both of whom were married. One of these was wed to Sir Ulrich MacWhirter, no doubt a relation, who had served abroad under the French king and who had received his knighthood from him. The other married a son of John, 2nd Lord Kennedy, by his second wife, Elizabeth Gordon, daughter of the Earl of Huntly.

When old MacWhirter died, both sons-in-law claimed the barony for themselves, stating that their wife was the elder daughter. However, by this time both had died, and no-one could vouch for any claim. To prevent a major feud breaking out, both men were persuaded to place the dispute before King James III, who was to decide the rightful claimant. At Edinburgh both put their case to the king, but so close were both claims that the king was unable to come to a decision. At length he arranged that a competition should be held to decide who should succeed.

Ulrich MacWhirter was given the task of running from Edinburgh to Blairquhan, and Kennedy thc task of riding on horseback to Blairquhan. Both would leave at the same time, and whoever arrived at Blairquhan and lit a fire in the great chimney would become the owner. At first the thoughts were that that the rider would have the easier task, but in those days the countryside was far rougher than it is today, and there being no roads the competition was closer than was expected.

Both men set off at the command, the king having left with some retainers earlier, so that he could see who was first at the castle. Sir Ulrich was accompanied by some men on horseback, to make sure that he did not cheat, but Kennedy was not, no-one being able to keep up with his fast gallop.

The story ends when the king was arriving at Blairquhan. Heading south from Kirkmichael he came over a small knowe above the Water of Girvan when he noticed the smoke rising from the uppermost tower in the castle. The king, knowing that Kennedy was behind, exclaimed, 'My kingdom to a bodle that yon reek is raised either by the devil or by his ain bairn, Ulrich MacWhirter.' Indeed, so strong was Sir Ulrich that he was able to reach the castle first and claim it for his family. The hill on the north side of the Water of Girvan has been known as the King's Hill ever since.

13.5 Blairquhan Castle was inherited by the winner of a competition. *(Dane Love)*

The story does not end there, for MacWhirter is said to have become something of a nuisance in the district, and it was resolved to get rid of him. He was replaced in the castle by his competitor, John Kennedy, whose family remained at Blairquhan until 1623, when it was acquired by the Whitefoords.

There is a long-standing traditional tale associated with a great cliff known as the Games Loup, which is located on Carrick shore, two miles south-west of Lendalfoot. The cliff is so steep and overhanging that the original road that made its way along Carrick shore was forced to find a way up the steep hillside and over Bennane Head before dropping to the raised shore at Ballantrae once more.

Sir John Cathcart was the laird of Carleton Castle, an old tower house whose gaunt ruin still stands by the side of Little Carleton farm. He was renowned for his number of wives, all of whom seem to have suffered strange and unpleasant accidents. Each wife Sir John took was an heiress, and not long after the wedding had passed and he attached her property to his, she seems to have suffered death by disappearing on stormy nights, apparently travelling when she shouldn't have. Eventually, over the years, seven of his wives were to succumb.

Sir John's last wife was to be May Collean, or Culzean, again the heiress to considerable property. Sir John took her on horseback to Games Loup one night, and there he told her that she was to drown like the other 'seven ladies fair; the eighth one you shall be.' Sir John told her to take off her clothes and jewellery, for he reckoned that they were too good and valuable to destroy in the sea. May Collean thought quickly and asked him to turn about, for it would be unmannerly for him to look at a naked woman.

13.6 Carleton Castle was the home of Sir John Cathcart, who did away with a number of wives. *(Author's Collection)*

Sir John was fooled, and when he turned round May Collean grabbed at him and threw him over the cliff. He fell into the sea, but he was able to plead to her to save him, and if she agreed he would return her to her father's gates. 'Nae help, thou fause Sir John, nae help nor pity to thee. Ye lie not in a caulder bed than the ane ye meant for me.' May was then able to mount the horse and return to her father's home.

13.7 Home of the Cathcarts for many years, Carleton Castle still stands in ruins above Lendalfoot. *(Dane Love)*

The tale of May Collean and Fause Sir John was written in ballad form, twelve verses in length, and was a popular rhyme for recitation at ceilidhs and soirees. However, the truth of the legend is more difficult to prove. There certainly was a Sir John Cathcart of Carleton, for he received a number of charters to his lands in 1485.

Within the Glentrool Forest, in the Ayrshire part of the Minnoch valley, lies the former shepherd's cottage of Craigenrae, in older accounts spelled 'Craigenreoch'. Located almost one mile south of Rowantree Toll, the cottage is now used by youth groups as an outdoor centre. About twelve hundred yards from the cottage, nearer to the Water of Minnoch, is a depression known as the Murder Hole. An old tale claims that a cottage hereabouts was home to a family of murderers. The story goes that a number of travellers, who were usually passing alone from Ayrshire to Galloway, disappeared, never to be seen again. Even their bodies failed to be found, despite intensive searches for them. Officers from local communities were sent to investigate, but even their inquiries drew a blank. A few stories began to circulate however, and one old shepherd relates how he had seen three people making their way across the moor, and only two returning. As the years passed many of those who lived on the moors began to move elsewhere, in fear of losing their lives, leaving only one old lady and her two sons, living remotely at Rowantree. She claimed that they were so poor that they couldn't afford to follow the others to safety, and was forced to stick it out.

One night a young pedlar was crossing the hill towards Galloway when he was beaten by the weather and the falling darkness. Anticipating a cold night out on the hill, he suddenly remembered the old woman and her cottage and determined to call there, where he was sure he would be able to receive some shelter. After a fairly arduous walk he came upon the cottage and arrived at the door. His attention was drawn by a noise from a lit room, and he peeked through the window. Within he saw the woman and her sons busily packing a large trunk, she sprinkling sand on the floor.

The pedlar tapped the window, causing the three to jump in fright. One of the sons ran to the door and grabbed the lad, dragging him inside. 'What do you want?' he asked.

'I am a lonely pedlar looking for shelter for the night,' he replied.

'Are you alone?' asked the old woman. When he answered in the affirmative, 'Then you are welcome,' she replied.

The lad was shown into a side room, where he was to sleep over night. When he lit a small candle and looked round he found the room to be in considerable disarray. The bed was partially broken, a chair had been knocked over, and some dishes lay broken on the floor. The door handle on the inside of the room was broken, and he realised that he would not be able to open the door for himself. The lad went to the bed and lay down, but he could not sleep. As he lay there he tried to work out in his mind what had happened in the room, but could come up with no logical explanation.

As the hours passed he suddenly heard a sound from the other room in the cottage. He walked silently to the door and was able to peer through a gap in the door left when a knot had dried up and fell out. One of the sons had a large knife, and he had just slit the throat of a goat. 'That was a much easier job than yesterday's,' he said. 'I wish all throats could be slit as easily. Was last night's slitting not a performance?'

The other brother replied, 'The Murder Hole for me. It makes for a cleaner job – you just slit their throats and drop them in. It's all by in a flash.'

The old lady interjected, 'What's it to be for him?' gesticulating towards the bedroom door.

The elder of the two sons lifted the knife and made motions across his throat.

At the sight the pedlar sprung into action. He bounded for the little window in the room, battered the glass from the frame and climbed through. Within seconds he was running for his life across the moor. The sound attracted the two sons' attentions, and they ran through the door after him. The pedlar ran as fast as he was able, even managing to outpace and lose the trail of the sons' dogs. Terrified, he continued running all night until he arrived at a small village. When he told his tale the residents were outraged. The men were gathered together and, armed with guns and other weapons, set off to Rowantree. At the cottage they found the old woman and the two men. Realising that they had no hope of escape, the murderers confessed to killing around fifty people and disposing of their corpses in the Murder Hole. The villagers took the murderers and hanged them from a tree that stood adjacent to their cottage. Another account claims that the murderers were taken to Cassillis Castle and hanged, the last people to be executed on the dule tree there.

The tale of the Murder Hole at Rowantree is one that has existed for many years, but there is no evidence of the existence of the murderous family. However, so good was the tale that S. R. Crockett, the famous Galloway novelist, took the story and relocated it to an even wilder part of the Galloway highlands. Crockett's Murder Hole, in his novel *The Raiders*, was located at Loch Neldricken, one of the high lochs that drain into Loch Trool. So established Crockett's tale became that modern Ordnance Survey maps indicate the Murder Hole at the west end of the loch, where a circular pool, almost separated from the rest of the loch, is claimed to be the place where the corpses were dumped.

An early account of the tale of the Murder Hole was included in *Blackwood's Edinburgh Magazine* of February 1829. In 1818, Alexander Murray, who lived at Rowantree, was asked by the historian Joseph Train, a friend of Sir Walter Scott and a native of Sorn, to investigate the depth of the Murder Hole. He used a length of twine and a weight, and from his plumbing of the depths he ascertained that it was around 80 feet deep.

Some of Ayrshire's old bridges have traditional tales associated with them, or at least stories that can no longer be confirmed by historical documents. The Auld Brig o' Ayr, which was made famous by Robert Burns in his epic poem, *The Twa Brigs*, is said to have been erected in the thirteenth century, but this may refer to an earlier timber bridge. In 1236 Alexander II granted a charter to the Royal Burgh of Ayr, in which a bridge is mentioned, and in 1440 the burgh charters make reference to it.

The old stone bridge that we see today, a popular footpath from the north side of the river to the High Street, is said to have two carved faces on the upstream parapet. These are now much worn, and are difficult to locate. The faces are said to represent two sisters, Marian and Mary Craufurd, who lived in Ayr sometime in the thirteenth century.

13.8 An old tradition explains why the Auld Brig o' Ayr was built. *(Author's Collection)*

Various accounts of the story place the date of the event at differing times. One claims the story took place in 1236, when Alexander II's charter for the erection of the bridge is known to exist. Others claim that the date was 1263, the year in which the Battle of Largs took place, when the Scots defeated the Viking invaders.

At any rate, the two sisters were in love with two men, soldiers of the realm. They were named Richard de Boyle of Kelburn Castle, and

Sandy Fraser. Serving their country, the men left Ayr to fight in some battle, either the Battle of Largs or some other conflict. The sisters remained in Ayr, fearing for their boyfriends. At length they decided to send one of their servants, Allan Boyd, to find out how they were getting on. A few days later he returned with the good news – the enemy had been defeated and the lads would soon be coming home. Boyd was given a purse containing some gold coins for his faithfulness and he was asked to organise a celebratory banquet for their return.

The two soldiers made their way back towards Ayr, but on their arrival at the river discovered that it was in full spate, the wet weather having caused torrential rain to fall on the uplands around east Kyle, and now it was tumbling in considerable flurry towards the sea. Undaunted, the men decided that they would risk riding through the brown waters, and so led their horses into the river. At first things went well enough, but almost at the same time the horses stumbled, and the riders were thrown into the swirling waters. The weight of their sodden clothing and armour pulled them under, and both were washed out to sea.

On the following morning the ladies were informed that their men had perished trying to cross the river, and that their bodies had been washed up on the shore. The maidens vowed never to marry thereafter, and they used their money to ensure that the same fate would never befall anyone again. The sisters paid for the erection of the stone bridge, and on the parapet their weeping faces were carved, recollecting their losses.

The tale of the two sisters has a number of other variations, and one account claims that it was a woman by the name of Isobel Lowe who awaited the return of her beau from battle.

The Old Bridge at Sorn probably dates from sometime between 1739-51, and it is said that it was erected at the expense, or at least encouragement, of the local minister, Rev William Steel. Prior to the bridge being erected parishioners had to use a ford to cross the River Ayr. Sorn as a village is quite new, the church being established in 1656 when Sorn parish was created from a larger Mauchline parish, and the present Main Street dates from 1780, when a local laird established a planned village. One Sunday, when the river was in spate, someone was drowned whilst they tried to cross the river in order to reach the church.

The minister was so distraught at the loss of one of his parishioners that he determined that this would never happen again. A fund was raised and the present old bridge was erected, a quaint hump-backed stone structure with a carriageway of only 9 feet 6 inches in width.

The Auld Brig o' Doon is another of Ayr's ancient bridges that has been immortalised in the works of Robert Burns. *Tam o' Shanter* is perhaps his greatest poem, an account of a farmer from Carrick who had become rather drunk following his attendance at the market in Ayr. His horse, Meg, was used to his inebriation, and often had to carry him home, knowing the route to go. Some of Tam's friends, however, had cut the hairs of the grey mare's tail, and when Tam sobered up the next morning he had to invent the tale of the witches of Alloway's haunted kirk in order to explain it to his ever-patient wife. The tale is too well known to recount in any more detail, other than to remind readers that it was at the Brig o' Doon that the witches were supposed to have pulled off the tail, just as Meg passed over the keystone of the bridge – witches being unable by tradition to cross running water.

The tale of Tam o' Shanter is either the figment of Burns' fertile imagination, or else his poetical working of a traditional story that was common in Galloway and Ayrshire in the eighteenth century. Tam and his drouthy crony, Souter Johnnie, were real folk, however, and they lived in the vicinity of Kirkoswald. Their graves can be seen in Kirkoswald kirkyard, under their real names of Douglas Graham ('Tam') and John Davidson.

Although the story is a figment of the imagination, there were some marks on cobbles on the approach to the old bridge that were supposed to have been made by the horseshoes of Tam's mare as it was furiously pursued by the witches. For many years people would point out the marks on the stone to children and would relate to them the story of Tam o' Shanter's mare. In the late 1980s renovation work was being carried out at the bridge, and the cobbles were lifted and relaid by the contractors. Unfortunately, no-one told them of the story of the marked cobbles, and they dumped them aside and relaid the roadway with different stones. Once it was noticed a furore erupted, and the contractors had to search for the original cobbles and have them replaced, where they can still be seen to this day.

Superstitious Ayrshire folk of times past often had various

traditional cures and remedies for a variety of ailments. Many of these were not unique to Ayrshire, however, being common across Scotland, but the following references are of Ayrshire examples.

The 'Evil Eye' was a common complaint in eighteenth century Ayrshire. One example is of a sick child in Galston parish. A 'doctrix' was consulted for her opinion and she declared that the cause of the child's illness was a near neighbour who had a 'bad eye'. The kirk session became involved, and the woman with the bad eye was called before it. She was ordered to go to the infant and say 'God bless the child.' A piece of the old woman's hair was to be cut from her head and this was to be used as a charm in assisting the child's recovery.

Similar accounts are given of people becoming ill due to the 'evil eye' being cast over them. One method of curing the illness was to make one's way to a point where two streams meet. From the waters seven round white stones or 'chuckies' should be lifted, and these were to be taken home and placed in a pot. Milk was added and the pot brought to the boil. It was reckoned that the milk boiled in this way and then drunk had miraculous curative powers.

Many farmers and other country folk held onto a number of superstitious cures for various ailments in cattle and other livestock. Many of these 'cures' do not appear to have any semblance of possibility to our modern ways, but in previous centuries these cures were regarded as being worthwhile. A strange superstitious cure, almost something of a sacrifice, took place on a farm in Muirkirk parish in 1670. James Hutcheone in Netherwood had a number of cattle who were suffering from some unknown disease. In desperation he resorted to an ancient 'grosse charme' which stipulated that he should cut the head off of one of his live calves with an axe. The head was then to be carried to a spot where two lairds' lands met each other where it was to be buried. This offering and burial was expected to prevent the disease from attacking the remainder of his cattle.

CHAPTER FOURTEEN

OLD CUSTOMS

There are hundreds of old customs that were at one time popular in Ayrshire that have died out in recent years. Many of these customs appear only to have been popular in certain parts of the county, whereas others were popular all over Scotland. According to John MacIntosh, writing in *Ayrshire Nights' Entertainments*, in 1894, 'Ayrshire people, like their compeers, have a select store of legendary tales and weird superstitions that date far back into the remote past.'

Some of the traditions and customs were associated with periods in the human life, such as births, marriages and deaths.

There was an old Ayrshire custom that was carried out prior to the baptism of a child. On the day before the child was due to be baptised, either the mother or a close relative of the new-born child would bake a special type of cake which became known as a 'Blythe-meet' cake. On the day of the baptism, as the new parents and their friends walked to the church, the person who was to carry the child was also given the cake. As they walked through the town, or along a country road, the first adult that they came upon was presented with the cake. This adult was then expected to carry the child for the next part of the way towards the church. This was seen as being an expression of goodwill towards the child as well as its parents. It was thought that the new-born child, who was said to have bestowed the gift, would have his generosity returned for the rest of his life.

Another tradition that was common was that on the day the child was being taken to the church for baptism, it should have its head covered with a white mutch, or head-cap. If the child did not have such an item covering its head then it was seen as being unlucky. Indeed, many females refused to carry the child towards the church unless it had such attire on its head.

The old Ayrshire method of becoming engaged to be married involved the couple standing on either side of a narrow stream. The couple would then bend down and wash their hands in the water, thus indicating that their intentions towards each other were pure. Once they had dried their hands, the couple would hold a Bible between them, over the flowing water, and would each swear a vow that thay would remain faithful to each other until death. The couple would then swap each other's Bibles, and thus they would keep them until the day of the wedding, when they would both return to the same house. This old custom, which appears to have lost its popularity at the beginning of the nineteenth century, was known as the 'Lovers' Vows'.

14.1 Robert Burns and Highland Mary may have performed a tradition form of marriage at Failford. *(Dane Love)*

A well-known example of the Lovers' Vows was when Robert Burns and Highland Mary parted for the last time by the side of the Water of Fail, just where it meets the River Ayr at Failford. In 1786 Burns and Mary Campbell had become lovers, following his estrangement from Jean Armour when her parents discovered his intentions, and the fact that she was pregnant by him. Burns met Mary, who was employed as a nursery maid by Gavin Hamilton at Mauchline Castle, and they became close friends. Burns had about the same time been offered a job in Jamaica and was intent on going, and so asked Mary to go with him and become his wife. In May that year they met by the side of the Fail and carried out the Lovers' Vow by the side of the stream. Mary was to return to her parents' home in Argyll to make arrangements for emigrating, but she was to die before she could return.

Robert Burns wrote about the Lovers' Vow, though he did not call it such, in a letter to George Thomson in 1792 – 'We met by appointment on the second Sunday in May, in a sequestered spot, by the banks of Ayr, where we spent the day in taking farewell before she should embark for the West Highlands, to arrange matters for our projected change of life.' Bibles were exchanged that day, for the Bible given by Highland Mary to Burns has been preserved, and can be seen at the museum in Alloway. What became of the Bible Burns gave to Mary is not known. In May 1921 a tall sandstone memorial was erected to commemorate the event by the Burns Federation, using funds gifted by Messrs. Harland and Wolff, shipbuilders in Greenock.

There was an old custom, noted in Galston parish, of how the lad obtained the permission of the lass's father to marry. The *Statistical Account*, written around 1791, noted that 'when a young man wishes to pay his addresses to his sweet-heart, instead of going to her father's and professing his passion, he goes to a public house, and having let the land-lady into the secret of his attachment, the object of his wishes is immediately sent for, who never almost refuses to come. She is entertained with ale and whisky, or brandy; and the marriage is concluded on.'

An old Ayrshire custom that was carried out prior to the wedding day was that of washing the feet of the bridegroom. The custom appears to have died out sometime in the mid nineteenth century, for it was noted as having 'become obsolete except in very rare cases' in 1894. However, John Warrick, writing in 1899, noted that it still lingered on in the Cumnock district at that time. Apparently on the night before the wedding the bridegroom's friends would make their way to his house and forcibly wash his feet. This old tradition altered somewhat when the men changed the custom slightly and used soot to wash his feet instead of soap. This probably explains the origination of what has become a 'blackening' in more recent years.

A Penny Wedding was at one time common across the county. The family who invited guests to the wedding party were usually of the poorer classes, and they would indicate that it was to be a 'penny wedding', or sometimes – no doubt once inflation had made a penny almost worthless – a 'pey' or 'pay wedding'. Guests would then make their way to the reception and would make a contribution towards the cost of the supper and entertainment. Once the fiddler, who was almost obligatory at such weddings, was paid for his services, and the cost of the food was covered, the money left was gifted to the newly married couple as an expression of goodwill. In the latter half of the nineteenth century the cost of attending a 'penny' wedding had become one shilling. The author's grandmother often used to talk of 'pey waddin's' taking place when she was young, brought up in the miners' rows at Cronberry, east of Cumnock, in the early twentieth century.

Penny Weddings caused the kirk some discomfort when they were initially in vogue, and much was done to try to prevent them. In 1694 the Synod of Ayr and Glasgow passed an act that repressed disorders and abuses at these weddings. The act was read from the pulpit and a copy placed in the session book. By the late seventeenth century it appears that these weddings had become too Bacchanalian to be acceptable to the kirk.

Shortly after a bride and groom were married, there was an old custom popular across the county known as 'riding the broose', sometimes 'riding the braize'. This was a horse-race carried on by the lads of the wedding party, who, immediately after the ceremony was completed, would race from the wedding place to the bride's new home. There the mother of the bridegroom was often in residence. The first to arrive would dismount and stand by the front door of the cottage, and would turn to face the arrival of the happy couple. The winner would have a bottle of whisky or wine, and the health and wealth of the couple would be toasted. The winner of the race usually received a prize. On some occasion the prize appears to have been the bride's handkerchief or a pair of gloves. The winner also had the honour of kissing the bride. The custom was popular at the time of Robert Burns, for he makes reference to it when addressing his auld mare, Maggie:

When thou was corn't, and I was mellow,
We took the road aye like a swallow:

At 'Brooses' thou had ne'er a fellow
For pith and speed;
But every tail thou pay't them hollow
Where-ere thou gaed.

According to William Gunnyon, writing in *Scottish Life and History in Song and Ballad*, published in 1879, 'the broose was generally ridden by well-mounted young farmers, tolerably mellowed with the national beverage, [and] it was a spectacle greatly enjoyed. When the bride reached the threshold of her future home, she was, like her Roman sister, lifted over it, lest she should stumble – a premonition of ill-luck; and a farle of oat-cake, or a weet-cake baked for the purpose, was broken above her head – a sort of silent invocation, that she might always have abundance of the stuff of life.'

A mention of the custom can be found in the *Courier* of 16 January 1813:

> On the 29th ultimo, at Mauchline, by the Rev David Wilson, in Bankend, near Cumnock, Mr Robert Ferguson, in Whitehill, of New Cumnock, to Miss Isabella Andrew, in Fail Mill, parish of Tarbolton. Immediately after the marriage, four men of the bride's company started for the broose from Mauchline to Whitehill, a distance of 13 miles; and when one of them was sure of the prize, a young lady, who had started when they were a quarter a mile off, outstripped them all, and, notwithstanding the interruption of getting a shoe fastened on her mare at a smithy on the road, she gained the prize, to the astonishment of both parties.

Riding the Broose appears to have died out in the mid nineteenth century, although there appears to have been an example of it taking place in Loudoun parish around 1880. Rev John Warrick, in his *History of Old Cumnock*, states that the last example that he was aware of it occurred around 1860, and that the race took the riders from the marriage at High Garleffin farm to the marital home at Watson farm. He states that a number of great feats were done on these occasions, but that also sometimes disastrous results could occur when accidents took place. On another occasion, in April 1845, when Lord Bute was married to Lady Sophia Hastings, the tenantry of Dumfries estate broke into a race for the house, much as they would at the wedding of their peers. Some say that riding the broose lost its popularity when wheeled coaches and better roads were created, the wedding party selecting to travel together.

Warrick speculates that riding the broose may have originated in the times when the bride was stolen by a disappointed suitor. Failing to win the hand of the woman by fair means, he resorts to foul, and arranges for a team of men to join him in order to kidnap her. This also explained why the mother of the bridegroom, who was not expected to attend the wedding, would be at the new marital home and would receive early confirmation that the bride had arrived safely and the wedding had taken place.

Another old marriage custom was that of 'creeling' the bridegroom. This custom appears to have been peculiar to the parish of Dalry, and was popular when penny weddings were in vogue. On the morning after the wedding ceremony, the neighbours of the bridegroom would make their way to his new home and grab a hold of him. They would then tie a wicker basket to his back, fill it with heavy stones and sods, and stick the shaft of a heavy broom into it, the branches of the broom facing upwards. Wearing this 'creel' the groom was made to run the gauntlet, passing through his neighbours. The only person who could untie the creel, and thus relieve him of his load, was his bride. It was said that the bride would untie the creel with a speed depending on how satisfied she was with him, the longer she let him suffer the less happy she was. Once the cords had been cut and the groom was freed of his burden, the gathering would make their way to the marital home and there consume the remainder of the wedding feast. New bottles of beer and spirits were produced, extending the festivities to a second day. It was noted by William Scott Douglas, writing in 1874, that the custom had changed over the years, but that at the time he was writing it had died out.

An earlier account of the custom is recorded in Galston in 1791. In the Irvine valley village, 'creeling' took place on the second day after the marriage. The young couple met with their friends at a convenient location. The creel was made for the occasion, and it was filled with stones. The young men present at the 'creeling' passed it between themselves, allowing themselves to be caught by the girls. Each time they caught a lad the girl was allowed to give him a kiss. After the young folk had their fun at this, the creel was handed to the newly-married lad. The young women left him alone, and he had to carry it for a long time, before his new wife took it from him, confirming that she had made the correct choice. After this had taken place, the company continued their merriment, dined together and then discussed the 'feats of the field'.

Rev George Smith, compiler of the *Statistical Account* of Galston, suggested that the French phrase, 'Adieu panniers, vendanges font faites,' may hint that there was a similar custom in France. This phrase was taken from Don Quixote, and roughly translates as 'good bye basket, the grapes can wait.'

At one time small parties erupted when the bridal party left the bride's home town, where the wedding took place, and before it arrived at the marital home, usually where the groom came from. Reference is made to a case in the early nineteenth century when a lass from Muirkirk married a lad from New Cumnock. After the wedding had taken place in Muirkirk, the party started walking the sixteen miles or so towards New Cumnock. At Borland, which is a few miles short of New Cumnock, the wedding party was met by a group of friends from New Cumnock. A fiddler was in the company, and he was asked to play a reel. In the middle of the road the company started dancing, all joining in. By the time they reached New Cumnock they were even more tired out than usual!

As with marriage, there were many customs associated with death and burial. When someone died in the district there was a custom of one person walking around the village ringing a hand-bell and announcing the death of the person. The bell-ringer would walk through the streets, ringing the bell, and shouting that so-and-so had passed away and informing the locals when the funeral would take place. The bell used for such a purpose was known variously as the 'deid bell', 'skellet bell' or the 'passing bell'. The bell looked rather like an old school hand-bell, the bell surmounted by a wooden handle.

At the funeral the coffin would be carried from the home of the deceased to the kirkyard by their close friends and relatives. The bell-ringer would walk in front of the cortege, ringing the bell, as far as the kirkyard. It is known that at one time the bell-man would be paid one penny per mile for his services. In the early eighteenth century, kirk session minutes record payments made for ringing the bell, such as:

> 1714: For Thomas Smith's wife's burial bell, £3 Scots [Kilmarnock].
> 1718: Received a crown for John Andrew's dead-bell, £3 Scots [Kilmarnock].
> 1762: Two pence per mile going in ringing the small bell – never to ring the small bell under two pence, and allowed two pence each for ringing the big bell [Galston].

Few deid bells are known to remain in Ayrshire. John MacIntosh, writing in 1894, states that at that time the deid bell of Loudoun Kirk still existed in the parish there. The bell was sent to the parishioners by James Campbell, 2nd Earl of Loudoun, who was at that time resident in Holland. On the edge of the bell the words *Loudoun Kirk* were cast in raised lettering. The hand bell used in Kilmarnock was inscribed *Kilmarnock 1639*, and was for centuries preserved in the town hall. Galston deid bell has the name of the parish and *1722* inscribed on it. The deid bell from Maybole had no markings on it, and is thought to date from the late seventeenth century. In 1911 it was on display at the Glasgow

14.2 The hand bell rung at funerals in Kilmarnock *(East Ayrshire Council www.futuremuseum.co.uk)*

Exhibition, after which it was preserved in the Kelvingrove Museum in the city.

Many residents of Ayrshire will state that women traditionally did not attend funerals, and that it was only in relatively recent times that they started so to do. However, women not attending funerals appears to have been a fairly modern custom, for in the eighteenth century there were a number of traditions associated with funerals that they would follow. It was noted that the poorer class of women would wear blue cloaks when they attended a funeral, and that the better classes would be able to afford red cloaks, trimmed with fur. According to the *Statistical Account* of the parish of Galston, written in 1791, 'it is usual for even the women to attend funerals in the village, drest in black or red cloaks.'

Burial customs were at one time extensive. Murderers, suicides and thieves often did not merit burial within kirkyards, or other sacred ground. It was common practise to have their bodies buried at cross-roads, or places where parishes joined, or else in banks that divided different estates. It was said that this was done so in order that the landowners could claim that no body of a murderer was interred within the extent of their property.

The festivities carried on at funerals could be excessive, and there are many early accounts of the amount of alcohol consumed at burials. On 1 March 1824 the kirk session and heritors in West Kilbride moved that they would 'discountenance expensive and unnecessary mode of entertainment common at funerals in this parish.' Similarly, in Kilmaurs, in 1793, it was noted that the cost of entertainment at funerals was considerable. Rev Alexander Millar, writing in the *Statistical Account*, opined that 'there is little merit in helping to bury those whom we help to starve. Nor do the deceased feel or enjoy any of the gratifications of vanity or misplaced veneration, which prompt this custom.'

In the *New Statistical Account*, written around 1837, various ministers noted their disgust at the amount drunk on these occasions. For example, in Old Cumnock parish, Rev Ninian Bannatyne stated that, 'it was very much the custom some time ago to give half a dozen rounds or more of spirits, wine, etc., at funerals; but there has been a decided improvement in this respect in recent years.' This improvement may have come about as a result of a covenant, or bond, drawn up by some of the parishioners, which restricted their behaviour at funerals. The original document is preserved at the Baird Institute Museum in the town, and reads:

> Covenant of Householders Regarding the Method of Conducting Funerals
>
> We, Subscribers, being in or near to the village of Cumnock, taking into our serious consideration that, by present method of conducting burials among us, much time is misspent and money thrown away, and that by entertainments given at many of them the Living are injured and the Dead in many cases dishonoured; and being convinced that a reform is necessary, have agreed and do by our respective subscriptions hereto annexed agree, bind and oblige ourselves to the Rules or Articles following, viz:-
>
> 1mo. That none of us shall give any general or public entertainment either immediately before or after the Burial of our friends, and that, exclusive of the members of our family and those connected with the chief mourner by blood or relationship, we will not invite any number exceeding 12 to partake of the refreshment that may be provided suitable to the occasion, which we hereby agree shall not exceed 3 glasses of wine, or where this cannot be purchased, one glass of spiritous liquors, and bread proportioned; Binding and obliging ourselves to pay a penalty of Five Shillings sterling in all cases where any of us shall be found to do otherwise.
>
> 2do. That in our Invitations to Burials we shall invite persons to attend punctually at the time at which it is intended to carry forth the corpse for interment, which hour being notified to the persons invited by the ringing of the church bell for so long a time as to allow the Invited to come from the most distant part of the village, the

> corpse shall be immediately carried forth to interment, under the penalty of Two Shillings in case of Failzie.
> 3tio. That the company invited shall be received at the Door of the House, where the corpse lyes at the time, by some of the relations of the deceased, with a Bow and Uncovering of the head, and the corpse being carried forth shall precede and the company follow to the place of interment.
> 4to. That, in order to carry the above specified Reform into execution such of the subscribers as may be judged best acquainted with the mode of Burials in Towns where they are properly conducted, shall, upon being called, cheerfully give their assistance to the same.
> 5to. That the fines raised and collected from Delinquents shall be applied for purchasing coffins and towards the necessary expense of interring the Poor in the village or neighbourhood, which fines shall be paid into --------, who shall be accountable for the same to any of the subscribers desirous to know in what manner they have been expended.
>
> These regulations we bind and oblige ourselves to observe, as witness our respective subscriptions at Cumnock, the 5th day of May, in the year 1800.

A total of 82 residents appended their signature to the document.

When a corpse was interred it was a common practise to hire what was known as a 'mort-cloth' to drape over the coffin. Coffins in olden times were not the highly polished crates that we have today, rather they were simple containers made from timber and unfinished. Accordingly, mortcloths were available from different sources, and these were draped over the coffin to hide its plainness. Today, the same sort of thing happens when a soldier or policeman is killed, and the flag is draped over their coffin as it is taken for burial.

Mortcloths were obtainable from different organisations, such as the kirk session or, in a number of parishes, from mortcloth societies, which existed purely to supply these expensive drapes. Society membership meant that the hiring of them could be paid up, thus allowing their use as desired. Often different qualities of mortcloth, perhaps distinguished by their age, were available, the newer and better looking cloth being dearer to hire. In 1771, for example, the mortcloths inWest Kilbride parish were available at five shillings for the best, and three shillings for the second best. These rates were increased soon after when a further cloth was purchased to eight shillings for the best, four shillings for the second and three shillings for the third. A child's mortcloth was also available at one shilling and tenpence. The new mortcloth acquired by the session in West Kilbride in 1788 cost a total of £14 1s to make, so they were expensive items.

Yet more old customs were popular at different times of the year, when the seasons change or the moon waxes and wanes.

The festival of Halloween is said to have had its roots in pagan times, and is supposed to be one of the oldest religious festivals that still exist. Today, however, most of the nonsense associated with Halloween has little to do with religion and is more a festival of witches, ghosts and other dressing up games. Even in 1894, when John MacIntosh wrote about the old customs of the county, he noted that 'Halloween is observed in industrial, matter-of-fact, Ayrshire, less and less every succeeding year, and the customs from which former generations derived so much harmless mirth, will soon be known only by name.'

On the week of Halloween a number of spaewives, or fortune-tellers, would roam across Ayrshire, predicting the future. They were often asked to tell when the daughter of the house would be married, and in many cases they seemed to be able to name who the husband would be. The spaewives were also in the habit of foretelling whether the union would be a fruitful and happy one, or whether the bride would live in unhappiness for the remainder of her life. In most cases, however, good fortune was predicted, for this would elicit better and more ready payments.

One of the old customs of Halloween in Ayrshire was to gather three nuts, perhaps acorns, and place them on the grate next to the fire. The observer names the three nuts after a lover, and they sit and watch as the fire burns. Should the nut crack open, due to the excessive heat, then this was seen as an omen that the lover whose name the nut bore would be unfaithful. Similarly, if a nut was to fall from the grate into the fire and be consumed, then the person after whom the nut was named would in due course be married to the observer.

Robert Burns makes reference to this old custom in his poem, 'Halloween':

> The auld gude-wife's weel-hoordit nits,
> Are round and round divided,
> And monie lads and lasses' fates
> Are there that night decided:
> Some kindle couthie, side by side,
> And burn thegither trimly;
> Some start awa' wi' saucy pride,
> And jump out-ow're the chimlie,
>   Fu' high that night.

Another old Halloween custom was for two girls to join hands, their eyes blindfolded, and to walk about the kailyard of the farm steading. When they found a stock of kail, or colewort, they were to pull this from the ground, and feel the root below. The shape of the root would indicate the approximate shape of their future husband, be it round and fat, or short and crooked.

Similarly, stocks of oats were also a good predictor of married life. A group of girls would make their way into the barn and there, in turn, pull three stalks of oats from the rick. If the third stalk did not have its top pickle on it, which is the grain at the top of the stalk, then the girl would not be a virgin when she went to the marriage bed.

Local traditions on Hogmanay tied in considerably with those practised across Scotland. It is interesting to note how some traditions have died out and yet returned, for if we read John MacIntosh's *Ayrshire Nights' Entertainment*, published in 1894, we find that the custom of wandering from house to house at 'The Bells' was at one time popular, but died out, and has returned:

> The subsequent visitations of first foots to the house of friends has, however, happily died away with advance of education and mental culture, and the orthodox bottle of whisky is no longer reckoned an indispensable requisite

> to the enjoyment of a New-Year's holiday. The questionable custom of open house on New-Year's Day received a death-blow from over indulgence, and is now more honoured in the breach than the observance.

MacIntosh noted that the gathering around the village cross on Hogmanay was still popular at that time. The residents of the burgh or village awaited the striking of the town clock at midnight, after which there would be cheers from the crowd. These midnight gatherings were popular all over Scotland, and certainly were so in Ayrshire. In Cumnock the residents gathered in the Square, to await the striking of the Old Kirk clock, after which there would be celebrating.

The waiting on the town clock striking midnight has died out across the country. It seems to have started to decline at the Second World War, when many of the sons of the parish were abroad fighting, and the decline was accelerated with the advent of television as a popular means of entertainment. People preferred to stay at home and await the striking of the bell (often Big Ben in London) before heading off to first foot friends and neighbours.

A number of border towns and villages still carry on the tradition of riding the marches. This takes place annually and is a custom whereby a number of appointed riders make their way around the boundary markers of the burgh, ensuring that no landowner or laird had encroached the public lands.

Riding the marches is a tradition that has died out in Ayrshire, but it was at one time fairly common across the county. Locally it was known as 'Redding' the marches, which is more akin to the local word 'red' as in 'red-up', or to tidy. In the olden times, prior to the establishment of fences, dikes and hedgerows to mark boundaries, the extent of various lands was difficult to determine accurately. At various locations boundary stones existed, in others watercourses or trees were used to mark the edges of properties. Sometimes these markers became lost or damaged, and it was the custom for the magistrates of various burghs to appoint twelve trustworthy young men, known as 'byrlaw men', to make their way around the boundaries of the burgh or parish and either check the boundary markers were still in place, or else erect new ones.

Kilmarnock at one time carried out the tradition of riding the marches each year. An old minute of the town council, dated 1710, notes:

> The said day it is enacted, statute and ordained by the Bailies and Council convened, that upon the last Munday of May instant, and that upon the first Munday of May yearly in all tyme hereafter, there shall be chosen by the bailies for the tyme, Twelve young men, who with such a nuber of the burliemen in the town, or the most old men as the bailies also shall condescend upon, shall visit and take inspection of the Marches in and about the whole lands to the town pertaining and belonging, and that what marches are wanting be set up and keeped in memory from tyme to tyme.

In Kilmarnock, a number of the inhabitants wished to witness the inspection of the boundaries, and formed a procession that followed the twelve appointed men. Many of the older inhabitants, often men who had been selected as the special dozen in the past, went on the ride to confirm where the markers had been in their day, thus ensuring that no encroachment had been made. According to Mackay, in his *History of Kilmarnock*, the old boys gave 'some of the boys who were present a hearty drubbing, so that they might remember in after life the identical situation of the said marches.'

The confirmation of the boundaries of the burghs was no idle pastime, for on many occasion the riders who had taken part were consulted when a territorial dispute took place. In Kilmarnock, in 1757, a group of riders were convened to settle a dispute whereby a fence or barricade had been erected on the edge of the Town's Ground. They had inspected the boundaries in the past, and were asked to confirm whether the adjacent landowner had tried to accede ground belonging to the burgh or not.

Many towns and burghs in Ayrshire, as in the rest of the country, had its own drummer or piper. The names of some of these people are still known, such as Matthew Bellamy, the last drummer in Ayr. The drummer was a popular person in the town as he was expected to wander around and spread the latest news. This was an important means of getting information long before the advent of radio and television. Indeed, it was said that it was the coming of the railway in the early nineteenth century that brought the custom of the drummer to a close, for by then news could be sent quickly across the country. In some towns the drummer also took part in riding the marches, such as in Kilmarnock, where he followed the procession, setting the pace by a beat. The Kilmarnock drummer also walked through the burgh beating the hide, to indicate notable days, such as Robert Cumming did in 1740, to mark the king's birthday. So keen must he have been that he broke the skin, and the burgh council awarded him £3 12s Scots to allow a repair.

14.3 The town drummer of Ayr, Matthew Bellamy, was an important figure in the town. *(Author's Collection)*

The town drummer of Beith gained some notoriety in the eighteenth century. He was James MacConnell, who argued with the minister of Kilwinning, Rev Alexander Fergusson, over some of the orthodox interpretations of the Bible. Fergusson libelled him for heresy to the Presbytery of Irvine, and the case was to be heard, but the minister died before the case was completed. MacConnell had been a soldier, serving with distinction for many years before being discharged. Around 1750 he married and settled in Beith, where he worked as a teacher. He was also the town drummer, constable and sheriff-officer.

The town drummer was usually regarded as an important man in the municipal organisation of the burghs, and as such was paid an annual salary. In Irvine, for example, in 1835 the drummer received a salary of £7, which was more than the town bell-ringer, who received £5 10s per annum.

In Maybole, the burgh councillors decreed in 1744 that all public announcements would be made from the steps of the town cross, located in the high street. The burgh drummer would stand there and beat the drum, known as 'tuck of drum', attracting the attentions of the townsfolk. Once the numbers who had gathered was sufficient, the proclamations were read. The burgh had to buy a new drum for the drummer in May 1774, for the old one was broken during a brawl in the street. In later years, Maybole's drummer became the burgh bell-man, a hand bell being purchased instead.

The ringing of church and town bells at certain times of the day was at one time a common custom across the county. At certain hours bells were rung to indicate different things. In Maybole, which was typical of the county villages, in 1772 the bellman had to ring the bell each night throughout the year at 8 o'clock, warning of the curfew. Similarly, he had to toll the bell in the morning at 6 o'clock to awaken the villagers. In later years, the curfew bell was rung at 10 o'clock in the evening. This practice ended at the time of the Second World War.

In Cumnock there was at one time a bell rung, or pipes played, at four o' clock every morning, apart from Sundays, to awaken the residents who required to travel some distance.

Dancing around the maypole is often regarded as being an old English tradition, one that did not take place in Scotland. This is not the case, however, for dancing around the pole was at one time a popular custom in this country, and it was popular throughout Ayrshire also. Maypoles were also known as simmer, or summer poles.

During the reign of Mary Queen of Scots, shortly after the Reformation, dancing around the maypole was prohibited by an Act of Parliament. This was because it was thought that dancing around the pole was heathen and the government of the time disapproved of drunkenness, mixed-gender dancing, and the general fun that they engendered. The act warned that 'gif onie women or uthers about simmer-trees sing and makis perturbation to the Queen Lieges in the passage throw Burrowes and uther Landward tounes: the women perturbatoures for skafrie of money or utherwise, sall be taken, handled, and put upon the cuck-stules of everie Burgh or Towne.' By the time Charles II had been crowned and the monarchy restored, dancing around maypoles had become popular once more. The tradition died out over the years, though Archibald Mackay noted in 1880 that it was still customary for youths in some parts of Scotland to 'go a-Maying' on the first day of May.

Reference to maypoles in Ayrshire have been found in Irvine, where in 1610 young folk of both sexes danced around it at the May holiday, latterly known as Marymass. In Kilmarnock in 1780, the town treasurer 'paid Robert Fraser, 2s. 6d. Sterling, for dressing a Maypole.' Writing in the *Old Statistical Account* of Maybole, in 1790-1, Rev James Wright noted that residents of the old burgh gathered around the maypole on the Ball Green and there played. He was probably in error when he states that the name Maybole was a corruption of Maypole!

BIBLIOGRAPHY

Adamson, Archibald R., *Rambles Round Kilmarnock, with an introductory Sketch of the Town*, Kilmarnock Standard, Kilmarnock, 1875.

Baird, J. G. A., *Muirkirk in Bygone Days*, W. Shaw Smith, Muirkirk, 1910.

Barber, Derek, *Steps through Stair – a History of Stair and Trabboch*, Stair Parish Church, Stair, 2000.

Baxter, David B., *The Parish of Largs*, Largs & District Historical Society, Largs, 1992.

Bayne, John F., *Dunlop Parish, a History of Church, Parish and Nobility*, Edinburgh University Press, Edinburgh, 1935.

Beattie, Frank, *Proud Kilmarnock: Stories of a Town*, Fort Publishing, Ayr, 2002.

Beattie, Robert, *Kilmaurs Past and Present*, Kilmaurs Historical Society, Kilmaurs, 1993.

Blair, Anna, *Tales of Ayrshire*, Shepheard-Walwyn, London, 1983.

Boyle, Andrew M., *The Ayrshire Book of Burns-Lore*, Alloway Publishing, Darvel, 1985.

Ayrshire Heritage, Alloway Publishing, Darvel, 1990.

Brown, Yvonne Galloway & Ferguson, Rona (editors), *Twisted Sisters: Women, Crime and Deviance in Scotland since 1400*, Tuckwell Press, East Linton, 2002.

Campbell, Thorbjorn, *Ayrshire: A Historical Guide*, Birlinn, Edinburgh, 2003.

Cuthbertson, D. C., *Carrick Days*, Grant & Murray, Edinburgh, 1933.

Autumn in Kyle, and the Charm of Cunningham, Herbert Jenkins, London, 1947.

Davis, Michael, *The Castles and Mansions of Ayrshire*, Spindrift Publishing, Ardrishaig, 1991.

Dick, Rev. Charles H. Dick, *Highways and Byways in Galloway and Carrick*, MacMillan, London, 1919.

Dobie, James, *Cunninghame Topographized by Timothy Pont 1604-1608*, John Tweed, Glasgow, 1876.

Douglas, William Scott, *In Ayrshire*, MacKie and Drennan, Kilmarnock, 1874.

Dunlop, Annie I., *The Royal Burgh of Ayr*, Oliver & Boyd, Edinburgh, 1953.

Gillespie, Rev James H., *Dundonald, the Parish and its Setting*, John Wyllie, Glasgow, 1939.

Gray, James T., *Maybole: Carrick's Capital*, Dragon Books, Bala, 1972.

Guthrie, Rev James A., *A Corner of Carrick*, Alexander Gardner, Paisley, 1979.

Henderson, Lizanne & Cowan, Edward J., *Scottish Fairy Belief*, Tuckwell Press, East Linton, 2001.

Hewat, Rev Kirkwood, *A Little Scottish World*, Stephen & Pollock, Ayr, 1908.

Ker, Rev William Lee, *Kilwinning*, A. W. Cross, Kilwinning, 1900.

Kirkwood, Rev J., *Troon and Dundonald*, Mackie and Drennan, Kilmarnock, 1876.

Lamb, Rev John, *West Kilbride: Annals of an Ayrshire Parish*, John J. Rae, Glasgow, 1896.

Larner, Cristina; Lee, C. Hyde, & MacLachlan, Hugh V., (editors), *A Source-Book of Scottish Witchcraft*, University of Glasgow, Glasgow, 1977.

Lawson, Rev Roderick, *Ailsa Craig: its History and Natural History*, J. & R. Parlane, Paisley, 1888.

Places of Interest about Girvan, J. & R. Parlane, Paisley, 1892.

Loudoun, Craufuird C., *A History of the House of Loudoun and Associated Families*, C. C. Loudoun, Kilmarnock, 1996.

MacArthur, Wilson, *The River Doon*, Cassell & Co., London, 1952.

MacIntosh, John, *Ayrshire Nights' Entertainment*, John Menzies, Glasgow, 1894.

MacJannet, Arnold, *The Royal Burgh of Irvine*, Civic Press, Glasgow, 1938.

Mackay, Archibald, *A History of Kilmarnock*, Matthew Wilson, Kilmarnock, 1848.

MacKenzie, Rev Archibald, *William Adair and his Kirk: The Auld Kirk of Ayr, 1639-1684*, Ayr Advertiser, Ayr, 1933.

MacNaught, D., *Kilmaurs Parish and Burgh*, Alexander Gardner, Paisley, 1912.

Maxwell-Stuart, P. G., *Abundance of Witches: the Great Scottish Witch-hunt*, The History Press, Stroud, 2005.

Normand, Lawrence, & Roberts, Gareth, *Witchcraft in Early Modern Scotland*, University of Exeter Press, Exeter, 2000.

Paterson, James, *History of the County of Ayr*, (2 vols.) John Dick, Ayr, 1847 and 1852.

The Ballads and Songs of Ayrshire, Thomas G. Stevenson, Edinburgh, 1847.

Pitcairn, Robert, *Ancient Criminal Trials in Scotland 1488-1624*, Bannatyne Club, Edinburgh, 1829-31.

Pugh, Roy J. M., *The Deil's Ain: The Story of Witch Persecution in Scotland*, Harlaw Heritage, Balerno, 2001.

Robertson, William, *Historical Tales and Legends of Ayrshire*, Hamilton, Adams, & Co., London, 1889.

Skelton, Douglas, *Devil's Gallop – trips into Scotland's Dark and Bloody Past*, Mainstream, Edinburgh, 2001.

Smith, John, *Prehistoric Man in Ayrshire*, Elliot Stock, London, 1895.

Statistical Account of Ayrshire, William Blackwood, Edinburgh, 1842.

Statistical Account of Scotland: Ayrshire, E.P. Publishing, Wakefield, 1982.

Steven, Helen J., *Guide to Prestwick and Vicinity*, Dunlop & Drennan, Kilmarnock, 1897.

Sorn Parish – its History and Associations, Dunlop & Drennan, Kilmarnock, 1898.

The Cumnocks: Old and New, Dunlop & Drennan, Kilmarnock, 1899.

Strawhorn, John, *The New History of Cumnock*, Cumnock Town Council, Cumnock, 1966.

The History of Irvine: Royal Burgh and New Town, John Donald, Edinburgh, 1985.

The History of Ayr: Royal Burgh and County Town, John Donald, Edinburgh, 1989.

The History of Prestwick, John Donald, Edinburgh, 1994.

Warrick, Rev John, *The History of Old Cumnock*, Alexander Gardner, Paisley, 1899.

INDEX

Figures in **bold** type refer to illustrations

W0006491